SACRED FOREST B...

"Ellen weaves spirituality, cultural connections, personal experiences, and science to transport you into the presence of the ancient forests. Her elegant writing flows with love of nature. This book gives us the opportunity to connect deeply with the wisdom of the trees and evolve our potential as human beings."

BEVERLY TEMPLETON, COFOUNDER OF GLOBAL TREE LOVERS

"Ellen Dee Davidson has devoted years creating a deep relationship with the redwoods. The living language of the trees is subtle; with Ellen's help, the gift the trees offer us is to learn how to enter into vibrant encounters with wise ancient trees."

ELYSE POMERANZ, TREE CONVERSATION
WORKSHOP LEADER AND WALDORF TEACHER

"*Sacred Forest Bathing* is a poetic invitation into one's own wild intelligence as part of nature rather than outside of it. Through Ellen's personal journey with the redwoods, we are given a field guide for our own encounter with the heartbeat of life. You will never see or feel life the same after walking in Ellen's hiking boots."

EDVEEJE FAIRCHILD, FOUNDER OF
A WOMAN'S NATURE SCHOOL

"A calming and much-needed balm in these chaotic, uncertain times. Journey with Ellen Dee Davidson into the ancient forests of Northern California and return home to the healing, sumptuous presence of the Standing Ones/Tree People our ancestors knew. You will be compelled to go outside and bond with your local trees and forests to rediscover the wisdom and healing energies of these sacred spaces. A must-read!"

MARE CROMWELL, GAIA MYSTIC, HIGH PRIESTESS, AND
AUTHOR OF *MESSAGES FROM MOTHER . . . EARTH MOTHER*

"*Sacred Forest Bathing* reveals how to receive wisdom and guidance from ancient forests where the interconnected web of life exists. A delight for the soul and an inspiration for the mind, this beautifully written book will resonate with anyone seeking affirmation of life's many relationships.

CAROL BROCK, FORMER EDITOR OF BOULDER MAGAZINE
AND BOULDER HOME & GARDEN MAGAZINE

"Ellen's clarity is born from decades of wandering the wilderness, communing deeply with trees, and researching ancient and contemporary Earth-based teachings at this time of planetary emergency. *Sacred Forest Bathing* is delightful, hard-hitting, compassionate, hopeful, and weaved together through Ellen's intelligence, sensitivity, realism, and utter delight for our living world."

JENNY SMITH, PRACTITIONER AT THE HAKOMI EDUCATION
NETWORK AND INSTRUCTOR AT ZENWAYS MINDFULNESS

"*Sacred Forest Bathing* is a journey, a meditation, and an initiation into myth, magic, and sensual communion with the forest. Ellen invites us into a world where the veils are thin and the wisdom of Earth and our primordial belonging here is undeniable. This book is her generous invitation for us all to come along with her into a multidimensional relationship with nature."

CHAMELI GAD, FOUNDER OF AWAKENINGWOMEN.COM

"With refreshing humor and humility, Ellen tells of falling under the spell of an ancient redwood forest. We are introduced to her favorite trees, learn about their vibrational energies, and experience the wisdom of their spirits. Along the way, we discover a path that can lead us to healing and wholeness."

MARY REYNOLDS THOMPSON, AUTHOR OF RECLAIMING THE
WILD SOUL AND THE WAY OF THE WILD SOUL WOMAN

"As we become weary and overwhelmed in an attempt to keep ourselves from becoming numb to the extreme suffering happening around the world, let Davidson be your guide to the life-giving powers of the natural world. She's a most excellent authority and counselor in leading us into states of awe, reverence, joy, and appreciation."

JUSTINE WILLIS TOMS, COFOUNDER AND HOST OF
NEW DIMENSIONS RADIO AND AUTHOR OF SMALL PLEASURES

SACRED FOREST BATHING

THE HEALING POWER OF
ANCIENT TREES AND WILD PLACES

A Sacred Planet Book

Ellen Dee Davidson

Bear & Company
Rochester, Vermont

Bear & Company
One Park Street
Rochester, Vermont 05767
www.BearandCompanyBooks.com

Bear & Company is a division of Inner Traditions International

Sacred Planet Books are curated by Richard Grossinger, Inner Traditions editorial board member and cofounder and former publisher of North Atlantic Books. The Sacred Planet collection, published under the umbrella of the Inner Traditions family of imprints, includes works on the themes of consciousness, cosmology, alternative medicine, dreams, climate, permaculture, alchemy, shamanic studies, oracles, astrology, crystals, hyperobjects, locutions, and subtle bodies.

Cataloging-in-Publication Data for this title is available from the Library of Congress

ISBN 978-1-59143-547-1 (print)
ISBN 978-1-59143-548-8 (ebook)

Printed and bound in the United States by Lake Book Manufacturing, LLC

10 9 8 7 6 5 4 3 2 1

Text design and layout by Priscilla Harris Baker
This book was typeset in Garamond with Autumn Embrace, Etna, Gill Sans, Legacy Sans, and Snell Roundhand

To send correspondence to the author of this book, mail a first-class letter to the author c/o Inner Traditions • Bear & Company, One Park Street, Rochester, VT 05767, and we will forward the communication, or contact the author directly at **EllenDeeDavidson.com**.

Ode to the White Barked Alders

What I have to share
Is the white-barked moonlit trees
Alders, bathing in rays
The bubbling spring
Fresh green moss
Rotting logs and moths
A habitat for fungi, snails
Slugs and salamanders
What I have to share
Is the foundational feeling
When soul connects to soil
And we breathe a sigh
Of presence in the organic
Balance of elements
Our bodies know
What I have to share
Is the way nature
Brings us home
In taste and smell and hearing
The caress of air on skin
So we feel the instinctual magic
Living grace
Of wild and holy places

Contents

Foreword

Allegra Moon

I am humbled and honored to put my voice into this foreword. To my amazement, Ellen Dee Davidson has the unique ability to paint her vibrant inner landscape with lyrical imagery. Her unique perceptions and innate wisdom will entice her audience to explore the profound healing that can occur while consciously being in the beauty of our outer world.

Her sense of reverence, humor, and glorious gift of imagination will land deeply into the hearts of readers. The desire to write and describe her adventures in *Sacred Forest Bathing* arose from a deep soul calling to share many of her experiences, which have profoundly changed her life. It is a journey that will affect anyone who is on a sacred path of self-exploration and desires to be assisted by the support of nature.

One can tune in to the subtle realms while being nurtured and held in the embrace of a wild environment, where our perceptions have fluidity to shift and evolve. Ellen's insights and awareness of her inner psyche are a true heart offering and a testament to the unique path that she passionately shares. Her wisdom floats like musical notes throughout a symphony of trees.

What started out many years ago as a magical game the two of us were playing in the forest has completely changed my life. One day, Ellen shared that the trees told her to "bring someone with her," and I have been in the incredibly lucky position to be that someone. The luscious beauty of the unspoiled redwood forest was so amazing that we felt like we were a fairy and an elf in the enchanted woods. During our joyous celebration in the outdoors, with nature as our guide, it seemed unimaginable that our daily lives would be affected in any tangible way by what we experienced in the forest.

We gave ourselves permission to play as we walked through the holy cathedral of the old-growth redwoods. We allowed the movement of each delightful moment to lead into the next. We meditated, took time to pause and listen to the birdsongs, and watched silently as butterflies flitted in and out of view. We put our feet in the cool creek and made circles on the surface of the water with our hands, before plunging our bodies down into the icy depths. We allowed ourselves to splash around in the vibrancy of the moment, completely captivated by the joy of the day.

There were many days while forest bathing when I felt like I was experiencing the most perfect day ever; a time so blissful, with my heart so open, that I wished it would never end. It was as if we were darting in and out of realms. My lively inner essence felt full of light. This was a way to explore the world with childlike curiosity and become completely captivated by the deliciousness of the moment. We were open, mesmerized, and totally immersed in a beautiful place.

What we did not know back then was that our lives, as well as the lives of our family members, would also change for the better. We became healthier, happier, and guided in our choices. We also began to notice coincidences. Often we would meditate and hear the exact same words, see identical images, or receive helpful information for each other and our families.

As we continue to explore forest bathing, we have witnessed many of the same subtleties. Some days in the trees are sweet, quiet, and supportive, which turns out to be the perfect remedy for calming our nervous systems. Other times, we feel ecstatic, celebratory, and filled to overflowing, witnessing the unbelievable majesty of the forest surrounding us. In contrast, right before the pandemic, we both had a similar vision of something slick and dark creeping and infecting the planet. At the time, neither of us understood what this warning meant, but we were unfortunately soon to find out about COVID-19. We have learned the importance of remaining open to whatever the energy, experience, and information is for that day.

Over time, our happiness improved. Dreams became more vivid. Our well-being continues to grow as we maintain our nature therapy spiritual practice. Like everyone, sometimes difficult situations and complications arise in our lives, but the support of wilderness increases our capacity to navigate the challenges that come our way. The wild path is a mystical path of embodied spirituality and continual growth. Nature play creates the opening for experiences to authentically occur, just as they are. In this way, we celebrate the beauty of Earth while reaching out beyond the stars and joyfully dancing with the elementals.

Sacred Forest Bathing is an opportunity to share in the magic of nature. The words dancing across the page have the potential to connect readers with their own higher guidance. My hope is that reading this book will open blessings into your life and that they will multiply in great abundance.

ALLEGRA MOON, owner of MoonImages Photography, has worked as a professional dancer, taught dance to children, and raised a daughter. As well as her highly developed kinesthetic senses, Allegra is also a gifted visual intuitive. She lives in the redwoods of Northern California and spends a lot of time in the forest opening her perceptions to the beauty of the trees.

Acknowledgments

Thank you to all the people who helped me with the creation of this book including those of you who are part of the story: my husband, Steve Davidson; daughters, Jessica Jones and Michelle Davidson; granddaughter, Stevie Alanna Jones; friends Allegra Moon and Annette Holland; teacher of embodied mythology Chameli Ardagh; founder of TreeSisters, Clare Dubois; radio show host Justine Willis Toms; soil scientist Michael Furniss; fellow tree climber Linda Melliner Smith; creator of a miracle forest Paolo Lugari; and founder of Archangel Ancient Tree Archive, David Milarch. I'm also grateful to everyone who helped me with the manuscript including: Elyse Pomeranz, Mary Reynolds Thompson, Allegra Moon, Faith Price, Carol Brock, Jenny Rose Smith, Edveeje Fairchild, Kathleen Brigidina, and Linea Stewart. Special thanks to Richard Grossinger for bringing this story to the attention of Inner Traditions. A reverent bow to the three lamas in the Tibetan Buddhist tradition who shared meditation techniques that helped me to connect more deeply with the trees. I was going to write my gratitude to the forest, but realized this whole book is a love song to the ancient redwoods.

An Invitation

These remnants of wilderness, places allowed to evolve
in their own wild ways without the interference of
human beings, give us glimpses into what it
feels like to be whole.

Imagine walking down a path on soft russet duff. The faint sweet fragrance of the simple, white trilliums with their yellow stamens wafts on the breeze. There are so many trilliums; they line the trail. The flute-like note of a hermit thrush punctuates the air, calling us back to this place and this moment in time, so our thoughts slow down and we start noticing more.

After this winter's fierce rains, the moss is scintillating with fresh vibrant aliveness. Waist-high ferns glisten with dewdrops. A blue jay flits through branches, flying between shafts of sunlight that seem to pour down grace.

It's so quiet here that the rustles of a chipmunk in the brush seem loud. It's so quiet here that we can hear ourselves think. It's so quiet here that we can hear ourselves not think. We can open up to the spaciousness and delight of being in a fragment of the wholeness that once was, a remnant of the glory of the biosphere Earth created over eons.

These remnants of wilderness, places allowed to evolve in their own wild ways without the interference of human beings, give us glimpses into what it feels like to be whole. And for sure it's not linear. All is curvy, fractal, interrelated. The essence of wholeness is when all of the disparate parts assemble in harmony, whether it is our body, emotions, spirits, minds, and essences or the elements of earth, water, fire, air, and space.

A common note in diverse ecosystems seems to be beauty; every environment has unique colors, scents, hues, vibrations, patterns, and energy fields that come together in exquisite coherence. Even the transitional environments, where we go from forest to beach, for example, do it with such elegance and interwoven delicacy that our hearts open to beauty.

My odyssey began over thirty years ago when my husband took a job in Humboldt County, California, in the far north of the state. It is a region of redwoods, rivers, and big lagoons along stretches of rugged coastline. There is even an old-growth redwood behind my backyard. I named the tree Grandmother Dragon Tree because she feels old and grandmotherly and has two prongs sticking out the top of her crown and a snout nose that resembles a dragon. (I'm calling the tree "she" because I can't bear to call living beings "it," as if they are objects.)

As soon as we settled into the house, Grandmother Dragon Tree began visiting and teaching me in dreams.

1992: Sleeping, the giant tree appears in my mind. She pulses with light and consciousness. I see waves of energy radiate from Grandmother Dragon Tree—up, down, and across the valley for a quarter mile in every direction. Words come into my dream. "My radiant field uplifts." And somehow I know she's improving the tone of all the life in this area: the creek and fish, occasional river otters, spawning salmon, eagles, hawks, herons, egrets, deer, bear, fox, porcupines, and myself and my family. Some nights in my dreams, I see starlight streak down her trunk, grounding into the soil. Other times, there is the vision of the tree, almost as if she is greeting me, and then the dream image of her morphs into pictures of mushrooms growing on her bark, huddled against her roots, or sprouting up in circles around her.

I can't figure out why the tree keeps showing me mushrooms. It is decades before I learn of discoveries scientists make about the importance of fungi and their mycelial networks transmitting nutrients between trees. At first, I don't understand the dreams at all. It never occurs to me that the tree is sentient and actually communicating with me. Instead, I analyze each dream in a Jungian way, as if the tree represents part of myself.

About fifteen years after Grandmother Dragon Tree's first visits to me in my dreams, I begin going on retreats and meditating with a lama in the Tibetan Buddhist Vajrayana tradition. The lama comes to my friend Annette's refurbished redwood barn. About twenty of us sit on woven wool carpets. During rainstorms, a woodstove keeps us cozy, while on hot summer days, with the windows wide open, we watch the crown sparrows dip and dive. Each retreat, we soften and open by meditating, dancing, listening to dharma talks, chanting mantras, and receiving the beauty of the blossoming rhododendrons. So I'm in a very receptive state when the lama suggests we "follow the juice."

I think he means that we follow our deepest heart wishes and do what increases our vital life force energy. Both of my children are grown and off to college, and I have more free time than I've ever had, so I start playing a game with myself upon waking and ask, "What is my heart's desire to do today?" Most free days, the answer is, "Go to the redwood forest." Although there is a lovely second-growth community forest in my town, Arcata, I can't resist the lure of forests that have never been logged and so usually drive either forty minutes south or north to find completely untouched redwoods. I begin hiking miles, sometimes with my husband, Steve, or one of my friends, most often

Allegra. I first met Allegra when our daughters were in elementary school and we were at an assembly. Looking across the sea of people, I saw her face lit up from within, glowing like a full moon, and it almost seemed like there was a twinkling tiara of sparkling fairy lights around her head. Later, she told me that I also looked luminous and magical, like an elf! We've been friends ever since.

But Steve is often busy with his garden, and Allegra with her family, so I usually go alone. Sometimes it is scary. I run into mountain lions, rutting elk, and black bears. But mostly it is blissful to be in all that silence, and I spend hours meditating with the old trees. I'm not expecting spending time in the forest to heal me, but it does and over the years I find myself happier and healthier than I've ever been. I'm also not expecting the spirits of the land to speak to me and to take me on a mythic journey that opens me up to visionary experiences, but they do and over the years I find myself increasingly able to receive the magical and mysterious wisdom of the trees.

Immersing myself deeply into the enchanted realm of the ancient redwood forest, I have discovered that everything communicates with me, often on levels too subtle to reach my conscious awareness. Information comes into my body, sometimes as an instinct—the way we often know who is safe or not, without understanding exactly why. Children and pets do this all the time. I've learned to trust this intelligence that permeates my body. When I don't invalidate what I'm receiving, things go better for me, and eventually I understand what I picked up. So I slow down and allow the trees to enliven me, awakening memories of a state of wholeness when redwood forests stretched from California to Canada, oaks were worshipped in my ancestral lands of Ireland, and people lived so intimately with Earth it was an entangled weave of life.

It still is an entangled weave of life. There's no getting around that. Modern humans have stepped back behind squares and rectangles, metallic devices, electronic barrages, noise, traffic, artificial perfumes, laundry detergents, and walls so that we create a delusion of independence, of not being entangled with life. But of course this is impossible. We are woven deeply into the fabric of Earth's creative expression.

We are in dynamic times where old systems are crumbling and we have yet to birth the new. It's a challenge to keep our balance and focus on what we do want, while feeling so deeply for our own and others' suffering. In this story of wild wanderings, I hope to explore ways nature can help us to lean into our fullness, health, and potential to get off this hamster wheel of human-induced suffering, abuse, and war on ourselves, one another, and nature.

We can look to wilderness for guidance, especially forests. Trees have been on the planet for over 360 million years. In that time, they have been huge contributors to creating the biosphere that has elaborated itself into this astonishing diversity of interconnected life. It's a stunning creation that has, in fact, made Earth habitable for us. We humans have only been here for a few million years, so it's safe to say trees are our natural elders. We can learn from them. As I take readers strolling down this wild path, I hope you, like me, will be reminded of your wholeness, the part of you that knows health, connectivity, and a way home to our original blueprint of living in harmony with Earth.

Before we wander in the woods, here's a little topo map of where this book is heading. Mirroring the diversity found in thriving ecological systems, *Sacred Forest Bathing* stitches together a tapestry of many strands. Woven throughout the book are myths and stories, scientific discoveries of the benefits of being in forests and other intact ecosystems, current issues we face like the climate and how a more conscious relationship with the natural world can offer solutions, and my living, breathing personal experiences of the healing and perceptually enhancing power of spending time in redwood forests and other natural environments. When we allow our empathy and imagination to open to the forest or any place in wild nature, we make ourselves available to an extraordinary realm of nature spirits and visionary guidance. We can receive mysterious and magical information and learn to co-create with nature.

Short chapters are set up in a way that conveys the sensual feel of being with the trees. At the end of each vignette is a brief Forest Guidance section giving readers more facts along with information about techniques and protocols to deepen their relationship with the natural world. Many include processes that can be done in a park, at the beach, the forest, in the mountains, a desert, or even at home with a houseplant.

For hundreds of thousands of years human beings have been connecting deeply with nature. We evolved outside in the varied ecosystems found on this planet, from forests to savannas, deserts to mountains and oceans. Our nervous systems are wired to be close to earth. It is our birthright.

Profound healing and expanded states of consciousness are possible when we enjoy more time in the countryside, especially if we do so in a mindful way. The combination of spending time with nature and practicing simple mindfulness techniques is more powerful than either one alone. When I began spending several days a week hiking and meditating in the ancient redwoods near my home, I had never heard of the term *forest bathing*. The words are a translation of the Japanese phrase *shinrin-yoku*, where the technique of immersing ourselves in the forest was first studied. Although I am incredibly fortunate to live close to ancient redwood forests and be able to be with them often, even a few days of being in a forest have been shown to lower blood pressure, decrease depression, lessen anxiety, and reduce stress for up to a month! Anecdotally, my friends and I have noticed that a day in nature also opens our perceptual and creative abilities.

I hope, dear readers, that this book will help you deepen your own connection with the vast intelligence and healing power of our astonishing Earth. In this intimacy, we are welcomed into the loving embrace of the mystery and beauty of nature. In this intimacy, we may find solutions we never imagined.

1
Health

Ancient forests are deeply healing.

*E*very opportunity I get, I'm out in the forests, rivers, mountains, beaches, and lagoons. Wilderness has healed me. For twenty years I was sick with fibromyalgia and chronic fatigue. I could hardly ever sleep, had painful muscle spasms to the point I could barely turn my neck, and my digestion was a mess. I was tired all the time while trying to raise my girls and break some epigenetic patterns of generational trauma.

When I first became ill, it was a gradual process. I was OK as a student because I slid through school without taking it too seriously or working too hard. When Steve and I were married, I felt more pressure to become a real adult. My sleep and digestion first became fragile when I took a job teaching emotionally disturbed kids. It was intense! Once a child tried to stab my hand with her pen. Another time one of the kids told me he was going to set me on fire. When I checked his file, I discovered he was there for having put kerosene around a sleeping man in a park and lighting a fire around him. It was so disturbing, and I was under constant pressure to apply behavior modification techniques, which was not my forte. For me, the worst part was that I'd dream with the kids at night. One night, I dreamed that two of the kids were psychic and I was afraid of them. The thirteen-year-old boy was throwing balls of lurid green and dirty red energy at me. I kept dodging, but was aware somehow that if one of the balls actually hit, I'd be immobilized and at his mercy. The next day when I went to school the eleven-year-old girl, who had been the second character in my dream, said, "You were in my dream last night along with [she named the boy], and we had psychic powers and you were afraid of us." She gave a sinister laugh and continued, "We almost had you." It was true and exactly what I'd dreamed.

So my health wobbled. I left that job and was better until I had my first daughter. The stress of being responsible for her well-being felt overwhelming, and she was colicky and didn't sleep. Soon, I also lost the ability to sleep. On a good night I'd snatch four or five hours. Many nights, I was up all night listening to guided meditations, doing yoga, drinking herb tea, and taking Epsom salt baths, but not sleeping. I never fell asleep during a nap either. It was a form of torture. I felt like jumping out of my skin. Becoming ill crept up on me with a cascade of increasing symptoms. My digestive system broke down first, followed by my ability to sleep, followed by muscle spasms.

My will to love my daughters and give them a good chance in life was so strong that, despite feeling ill, we somehow made it through and it all turned out well. We are happy together. Love is strong medicine. We also had Steve. He worked a lot, so most of the childrearing was on me, but he has always been loyal and steady as a rock. We could rely on him without question.

I cut out most of the activities in my life that weren't absolutely necessary and lived simply—taking walks, cooking, cleaning, and chauffeuring my daughters wherever they needed to go for their many activities. I didn't have the energy to have much of a social life. About ten years into the sleepless torture, I discovered tranquilizers actually helped. I used them sparingly, afraid of addiction. That worked for a decade until my youngest daughter's appendix ruptured, and she was in the hospital for ten days, during which time I used tranquilizers every single night. When I tried to stop, I could not.

Until I spent time in the redwoods.

Ancient forests are deeply healing. Spending time in forests is proven to accelerate physical wound healing, hasten recovery from surgery, and help kids with ADHD focus. These benefits are not only due to the serenity of the forest but also to chemicals called phytoncides, which trees put into the atmosphere to protect themselves from insects and fungi. Phytoncides are antibacterial and antifungal and stimulate our bodies to increase the activity of a type of white blood cell called natural killer cells, which attack cancerous and virus-infected cells.

Being in the forest likely boosted my damaged immune system. But more than that, it embraced me: I was held and soothed in the sheltered environment of the trees. Beauty opened my heart and filled me with gratitude. I bonded deeply with Earth, feeling held by Gaia's gravity, expanded by her beauty, and filled with elemental grace that enlivened my cells and made them sing.

Similar to the way my illness crept up on me with one symptom leading to others, healing happened by mending one broken system after another. This is a well-known phenomenon in energy medicine practices, such as acupuncture, reiki, jin-shin jyutsu, chi-gong, and homeopathy. When they work, the effects don't exclusively cure one broken part of the body but manifest throughout in beneficial ways. I knew that. What I did not know was that being within the forest was energy medicine.

Improvements to my health were gradual. I felt more peaceful. I slept a little more. Many mornings I awoke eager and excited to go to the trees. I felt overwhelmingly grateful to have the time to visit the parks, the car to drive me there, enough money for gas, and a lunch. Bit by bit, I healed until now, at sixty-nine, I feel remarkably well.

Sitting with the trees rewired my nervous system. Spiritual

guidance came through, as if the trees were connecting me to divine nature intelligence. Over and over again, I was shown my next healthy step, until I learned to trust the universe and live one step at a time, following my intuition and heart wishes. Slowly my body, mind, spirit, and emotions mended in one of the few forests on Earth that have never been interfered with by human beings.

Recalling how I became ill with an almost domino effect of symptoms, one leading to another and all of them exacerbating each other, and then how I have healed has given me a model of how our environments can also be restored. My healing journey was the reverse of the one I took on my way into chronic illness. As each system in my body improved a little bit, others would also spontaneously improve. They are all interrelated, similar to the way ecosystems are intricately woven together. Unravel one, and others are strained and sometimes come undone.

As we humans put efforts into restoring environments ravaged by our misunderstanding, ignorance, greed, and generally out-of-balance lifestyles, we can start anywhere and discover it has beneficial effects for the whole. Protect clean water, and it will continue to nourish soil. Clear the air, and plants will have an easier time breathing. Plant more trees, and they will keep the soil from eroding. There's no place too small to start, and that includes taking care of and being kind to one another. Every little effort counts.

And so now I am off on this gorgeous spring day to frolic in the woods with my friend Allegra. We can't wait to find out what the trees will share today.

Forest Guidance

Our health is inextricably linked to the health of our environment. We need to protect both. Allow yourself to witness what you are called to care for. What are you guardian of? It doesn't have to be something huge. You may be guardian of a child, a relationship, a pet, your own sleep, or a particular tree or stream. Settle into your favorite spot in nature and ask, "What am I guardian of?" Perhaps you are a guardian for that particular place. If you are drawn to do so, use your nondominant hand to write the answers you receive. This will help you to connect to the intuitive side of your brain. A few more questions you might ask are, "What is my next step in this guardianship?" "What support or healing do I need in order to be effective?" "What else am I guardian of?"

2

The Goddess Beauty

How do we water the seeds of the world we want?

Today, Allegra and I are hiking through the blooming yellow skunk cabbages, nestled into the wetlands like a Monet garden. Their pungent spicy smell fills the air. Winter wrens sing overhead. Every once in a while, I spy a small brown bird tucked in and partially hidden, like a little mouse snuggled into the roots of a fallen tree. Winter wrens are so plain compared to the magnificence of their songs, which fill the air with the joy of spring. Ah, to be alive to witness another spring! I sing along with the birds. One wren pauses her song as if listening and then sends another musical phrase shimmering through the forest.

Laughing, I romp down the trail. Spring is so vibrant that I can feel the plants delight in bursting growth. It makes me feel young. Beauty opens me to childlike wonder. Beauty is, herself, a goddess. She's sensual, enticing, and lures us in with her attractiveness. She's the most natural being in the world. Everywhere, nature creates exquisite beauty, whether it be rivers, deserts, rocks, mountains, forests, clouds in the sky, oceans, or canyons. Beauty is easily found in all ecosystems.

Beauty brings us home. We want to notice her, and that gets us right here, living in the present moment, the way so many spiritual teachers have recommended. Beauty is my easiest path into the now.

I'm not the first one to notice the potency of beauty. Artists, poets, lovers, and many of us seeking a creative muse have been inspired by beauty. Tasting the tip of a tender fiddlehead fern, I think of how utterly sexy spring is. Plants are plump and juicy, colorful and enticing. If I were a bee or wasp, the yellow stamens of the white trilliums would be impossible to resist. Even to me, they look delicious.

To me, trilliums seem like the unicorn of flowers: rare, pure, elegant, and ethereal. The facts about them make them seem even more mystical. Each flower yields one seed per year, but the plants can live for almost twenty-five years. Still, it takes nine years after germination for a single trillium flower to bloom.

Perhaps most amazing is that the ones found in the ancient redwood forest, *Trillium grandiflorum*, are given their start in life by ants! Attracted by the sweet coating covering the seeds, the ants carry them underground into their colonies. They have been seen carrying the seeds as far as thirty feet away from the original plant. Once the ants have feasted on the sweet coating, the seeds are put on the ant compost pile and left to grow in a perfect underground environment. No wonder my trail is literally lined on both sides with trilliums.

Putting my nose a few centimeters from the flower, I inhale a fragrance too exquisite for words—although I'm a writer, and so I try. "It smells like an understated plumeria blossom," I tell my friend.

"Much more delicate," Allegra replies.

I agree, continuing to think about the goddesses of beauty. Freyja pops into my consciousness. I've been part of an Awakening Women Sadhana offered by Chameli Ardagh, and we are delving deep into the mythology of Freyja. There are many definitions for the word *sadhana*, which is a Sanskrit word roughly meaning "going directly to the goal of realization through spiritual discipline and various practices." One method to do this is to evoke and embody the qualities of a deity. In spring 2023, I attended an online twenty-one day experiential sadhana, led by Ardagh, during which we embodied Freyja's qualities. This was easier to do for me with Freyja than it had been with the goddesses we'd previously studied, such as Inanna. Freyja felt like me! She's a majestic Nordic nature goddess, sensually alive, patron of the feminine mystical arts, untamed and free and loves the forest.

Forest goddesses have arisen in cultures all over the world, wherever trees can be found. My maternal Celtic ancestry has quite a few including Flidais, the Lady of the Forest, who guards fauna and flora. In the eastern Baltic, there is Lauma, a woodland fae goddess of trees and marshes. A Yoruba goddess named Aja is an Orisha spirit of the forest, kindred with animals, who heals with herbs. Some goddesses, like Arduinna, are specific to a particular forest, in her case the Ardennes forest region in Belgium, Luxembourg, and France. Asherah is a Jewish tree goddess. Kurozome is the spirit of the Japanese cherry tree. The Dakota and Lakota tribes honor Canotila (Chawn-oh-tee-lah), which means "little tree dwellers." Even Aphrodite, most often known as the goddess of love and beauty—the word *aphrodisiac* comes from her name—is also a nature goddess associated with apple trees.

Many of the tree goddesses are also goddesses of beauty. Dancing down the trail, arms waving as if I have more than two, like the Tibetan goddess Tara, who is also the goddess of beauty, I think of how I wrote about my own forest goddess of beauty, Dania, in *Wind*, a children's ecofantasy book. She is my personal takeoff on the Roman goddess Diana. Appearing in my imagination for decades as the Golden Lady with the Lion, Dania can shape-shift into a tree. Like many goddesses, Dania expresses qualities that I can find within myself. She is the part of me that is strong, confident, and a protector of wildlife. When I am sitting in the trees, it is easy for me to conjure this goddess in vivid detail. Absorbed in the curvy, leafy, sensuous loveliness of the forest, it is so effortless to imagine Dania that sometimes I feel like I'm with my forest goddess of beauty.

Our culture still worships beauty but, as with so much of the sacred, in a diminished and profaned way. Instead of the irresistible, healthy attractiveness of blooming as who we are, we have been taught that we have to change. Too fat, too thin, too old, too young, too this or that. In an effort to please, we twist and contort, losing the clear expression of ourselves that is inherently beautiful.

We've lost the goddesses we are.

Free.

Fierce.

Authentic.

Walking down this trail, I feel free, fierce, and authentic. Gaia comes to me, robed in redwood trees, towering over three hundred feet above me, some thousands of years old. She comes to me in the breath of scented air, the humming song of the forest, the caress of soft zephyrs on my cheeks. She comes to me in sweetness flowing into my heart. Gaia comes to me as a goddess, and this is one goddess of beauty I can get to know directly. I smell, hear, taste, see, and touch her. My perceptual capacity opens, and I know her through time, through the causal level, through the holographic blueprint that glistens energetically in my mind's eye before taking form in matter. The seed knows the flower before the flower arises.

How do we water the seeds of the world we want? How do we create the conditions for beauty to flourish? How do we allow our own beauty to shine forth?

Forest Guidance

Take in the beauty of natural surroundings by focusing on your senses. A mindfulness activity that has helped me is to notice five things I see, such as colors, shapes, patterns, objects, and the quality of light; four things I feel, like the air on my skin, the smooth or rough bark of a tree, my feet on the ground, and the clothes I am wearing; three things I hear, including birds, water, the wind in the trees; two things I smell, which might include the sap from trees or the fragrance of flowers; and one thing I taste, which could be a berry, a sip of water, or a plant like redwood sorrel. This practice can be done anywhere and is great for helping us ground and become more aware of where we are in space. When we do it in wild environments, it is delightful.

3
How Do We Listen?

I never quite catch the moment when it becomes
tree and me, me and tree.

One way to allow our beauty to shine forth is to become more present, and we can do this by learning to listen. Listening is a capacity of presence. The more of ourselves and our full attention we bring, the deeper we are able to receive what is being communicated. This is true in our relationships with people as well as plants, trees, rocks, rivers, mountains, animals, birds, and insects. It's probably true for the stars. Have you ever stared at one particular star so long that you felt you could hear the star song?

In order to be present, we have to let go of all the distractions, let go of the ceaseless monkey mind thoughts. This isn't always as easy as it sounds. Usually, I sit with the trees for two hours, and the first hour is spent mostly settling before I feel calm, clear, and present. I don't try to stop my thoughts; I let them be, watching them come and go and catching myself when I find myself following one along a thought train down the rabbit hole of somewhere else. Focusing my attention on something, like my breath, the view, the sound of the water, or bodily sensations, helps. Our bodies are always right here, right now. They do not exist in the past or future. Trillions of cells are each receiving myriads of information in all sorts of ways: nutritional, electrical, spiritual, vibrational, emotional, biochemical. Most of this happens without our conscious awareness.

To function, we screen out most of reality.

When we want to experience our deep connection to nature, all we have to do is slow down into what already is. We are one aspect of nature evolving within the greater matrix of life.

As species morph and change in response to altering conditions, the natural world continues with an endless display of creative, evolutionary expressions. Mother Nature reveals artistry at every turn, expressing through patterns. From pine cones to ice and snow crystals, from rivers to our lungs that resemble the branches of trees, we see repeating fractals. My favorite example is a tree. Each branch looks like a smaller tree with the Y shape occurring over and over again. Even the leaves are fractal, with midline veins that resemble the trunk of a tree and smaller veins branching out.

Like nature's art, our human creativity often tends to repeat the same images and themes. We evolve not by moving forward in a straight line but by returning again and again to what matters most to us, evolving and growing by going deeper and deeper into familiar territory until we uncover something fresh. Life is nature's art, and we are part of that life.

So how do we humbly come back to our place in the great artistic web of being? To begin having nature therapy experiences, the first thing is to discover a spot close to where you live so that you can return at least once or twice a month to experience the full effects. It doesn't have to be a forest. A meadow with the enticing fragrances of flowers, a mountaintop with the radiance of powerful rocks, or a beach with the sound of waves lapping the shore are some of the many environments that can offer us the healing experience of nature immersion.

Once you have found an enticing spot where you feel safe, set aside a few hours. At least two hours is needed to receive the full benefits of nature therapy, and it is essential to turn off cell phones and other devices. Be sure you know the hazards of the location before beginning so that you can protect yourself from sunburn, dehydration, cold, poison oak or ivy, animals, pollen, and ticks, which can cause Lyme disease.

With ticks, the trick is to wear light-colored clothes so you can see the reddish-black body of the tick. Tuck your pants into socks and wear a long-sleeved shirt. Do a full-body tick check after your outing. My doctor told me that ticks have to dig under your skin for a minimum of thirty-six hours to cause disease. If you are uncertain how long a tick has been attached and are concerned about contracting Lyme, you can take the tick to a local public health laboratory and have it checked. It's good to know because antibiotics are effective when given within seventy-two hours of a tick bite. Knowledge keeps us safe to explore the rejuvenating properties of time in nature.

When you have found your spot and turned off your phone, slow down. Take in long, deep belly breaths. If it helps, breathe in to the count of five, hold for five, and breathe out for another five counts. Begin by centering yourself in the same spot for five to fifteen minutes, soaking in the atmosphere. Notice what you smell, the colors of the leaves or stones, the texture of bark or water. Ecotherapy evokes states of awe, wonder, and gratitude. These states of consciousness help us to heal.

For people who want more guidance, there are certified forest guides through the Association of Nature and Forest Therapy (ANFT). Guides can help you find suitable trails and learn how to tune into your senses. Be aware of the rules in your state and national parks. When I looked into taking people forest bathing in the redwoods, I was informed by the California State Park system that it is illegal to charge anyone to take them to a park, not even to split the gas to get there, without first acquiring a special permit. Personally, I love this rule, which prevents commercializing nature's holy cathedrals.

If you are someone who loves to track your healing progress, you may want to check your blood pressure, pulse, quality of sleep, and mood before you go. After you return home, you can check again to see if there are any improvements.

Although I usually hike miles before settling down to sit for a couple hours with an old-growth redwood, this is not necessary. If you love exercise, want to get a more expansive feel for the lay of the land, and feel great after a long walk, by all means hike first, as I do. For most people a short half-mile stroll into the forest or other environment is all that's required. Enter your chosen place with reverence. Be silent and still. Take a moment to be aware of your surroundings. When I do this, it usually feels quiet and peaceful, but every once in a while I have a vision.

Today I have the permit to go behind a locked gate and down a dirt road and hike a little over a mile to a grove of magnificent redwood trees. To me this feels like the heart of the realm, a fairy-tale environment of giant ferns and huge trees bordering a jade-colored creek that can look like a raging river after a winter storm. One redwood tree is on a bluff overlooking the river. Whenever I sit with her, I feel the stars shining down on me, even though it is usually daytime and I can't actually see stars, so I named this tree with her straight trunk Star Tree. At the time I named her, even though I'd received five Tara empowerments (a Buddhist practice that gives initiates vibrational entry to working more deeply with various deities), I had no idea that the name Tara is derived from the Sanskrit root *tar*, which means "tree," "to cross over," and "star." But somehow my body must have perceived this relationship between trees and stars and how trees can help us cross over into cosmic consciousness.

Sitting close to Star Tree, in my mind's eye I see light shimmering down her trunk, through my physical being, and into the soil. In some enigmatic way, my presence seems to help the tree ground the starlight.

I'm not the only one experiencing the relationship between

Earth's magnetic fields and living systems, including the relationships between trees and people. HeartMath Institute has been studying the interconnectivity between human beings and trees through its Interconnectivity Tree Research Project. According to anthropologist David E. Young, in his book *The Mouse Woman of Gabriola*, the energy found in waterfalls, rocks, animals, and trees is called *mana* in Polynesia, and in Japan this divine power is known as *kami*. In Japan, certain sacred trees are revered for being full of the healing power of kami.

Druids in Ireland considered all trees to be sacred, especially oaks. In the Kabbalah there is the Jewish Tree of Life. Norse mythology includes a world tree named Yggdrasil, which the nine worlds exist around. There are obvious reasons why many cultures around the world have revered trees: they provide fruit and nuts, wood for hearth fires and homes, shade, oxygen, and fresh water through transpiration. In this process trees pull water up through their roots, use as much as they need, and then release the rest of the moisture into the atmosphere through tiny, microscopic holes in their leaves called stomata. Trees and plants have literally made life on Earth possible for us. Druids performed holy ceremonies around trees, celebrating changes in the seasons and the phases of the moon.

Although kami, mana, and the energy Druids and others have perceived around sacred trees have common healing and uplifting properties, it's likely that the flavor of each emanation varies a bit from culture to culture and tree to tree. No two living beings on our planet are ever exactly the same, and neither are their auric fields. While I do feel something similar to kami or mana in the presence of old-growth trees, I've noticed that there are subtle differences between individual redwood trees within the same forest. Each tree seems to radiate a singular essence. Even the same tree is not the same in every season or even on every day. And neither are we. Like any intimate relationship, the interaction varies depending upon our own state of being as well as that of the tree and the entire entangled Earth-cosmic relational moment.

Sometimes a tree's energy is more internal and does not feel as available. Other times there is a sense of invitation, a warmth in our hearts, a welcoming embrace. Occasionally, the healing energy a tree exudes is as palpable as sweet, thick, golden honey, and we can bask in the healing balm. Often we will feel a sense of peace. These feelings of well-being can stay with us for a good while after a day in the forest. For me, there's a sense of calm and a feeling of being held. I relax. It's remarkable how much healing simply relaxing brings. It certainly has improved my sleep!

Today, with Star Tree, my heart beat slows. My pulse comes into rhythm. I breathe more deeply. Smells are vivid. Senses enliven as my animal body stretches and moves, finding the most comfortable position. Careful not to trample any roots, because the roots of redwood trees can be harmed when weight is put upon them, I snuggle comfortably with my back, head, and hands near the trunk. I used to sit right against the tree, but with more people visiting the redwoods I am concerned that so many people sitting against the trunk will rub moss, lichen, and bark off or disturb the tree in other ways. I've found it isn't necessary to actually touch the tree to bathe in the radiant field of a redwood. Being within a few feet of the tree can plug us into the energy. For me, it feels electromagnetic, and there is a tingling warm current from my skull to my toes. I am being healed, and neck muscles that have been tense for years spontaneously twitch and tingle, releasing tightness I didn't even know could be released so that I can turn my head without pain.

I never quite catch the moment when it becomes tree and me, me and tree, but there's a sensation of my blood flowing like sap, of moving through both the heartwood of the tree and the fibers of my own heart, of a knowing that is greater than my own knowing alone.

Forest Guidance

Our bodies pick up far more information than our minds can consciously process, so it is a good practice to listen deeply to our bodies. Is your breath fast or slow? Are you aware of your toes? Are you jittery and anxious, sad or upset, or contented in this moment? Is your stomach clenched and tight? What is your belly telling you? Allow all your emotions to flow, honoring the way you feel. In a forest or other natural setting, we can simply be, witnessing ourselves exactly as we are. I've found being present with how I actually feel helps me to tune more deeply into my surroundings. Maybe this will be true for you as well. See if accepting yourself as you are in this moment helps you open to receive all that the forest, sky, sea, or houseplants are offering. As we learn to rest into ourselves and our environments, we become more connected to nature. One practice that has helped me is deep listening, both to myself and nature. Jenny Rose Smith, who trained in Carl R. Rogers's techniques for active listening and the Hakomi Method, has developed a meditative and psychotherapeutic approach called Receptive Listening, which I have found effective. She offers weekly online deep listening support sessions.

4

Angel Trees

Although I still clutched branches as if my life
depended upon it, there was a heady joy
in being up so high, on top of the world.

My bond with trees grows even stronger when I connect up with David Milarch, founder of Archangel Ancient Tree Archive (AATA). Like many people, I first heard of David when I read Jim Robbin's book *The Man Who Planted Trees*. Inspired by AATA's work creating Living Tree Libraries around the world, I donated twenty-five dollars a month to the nonprofit organization. Much to my surprise, David contacted me.

Figuring David couldn't possibly have time to talk to everyone who donated small sums, I asked him why he had emailed and then called. "Everything I do for this project is guided by archangels," he replied, "including talking to you."

His story of how he met up with the archangels is incredible.* After growing up on a shade tree farm in Michigan, getting married, and having two sons, David had a near-death experience. While he was officially dead, he found himself in the most beautiful place imagin-

---

*This story and others from David Milarch are from interviews I had with him in person at Jedediah Smith Redwoods State Park as well as by email and phone, from 2012 to the present.

able, feeling musical harmonics go through his whole spirit body and watching a gorgeous sunrise. He never wanted to leave, but the archangels told him he had to go back and clone the oldest champion trees and plant them in Living Tree Libraries around the world. A champion tree is the largest specimen of its species. These mature trees are especially hardy, having endured for hundreds of years to achieve their impressive sizes. At the time of David's vision, old trees had never been cloned before, and people told him it was impossible.

Decades ago, when David first began his mission from the archangels, it had not yet been proven that the genetics of the old champion trees were important. People asked, Why not plant any old tree? Now science has confirmed that genetics do matter; old champion trees are better able to withstand the rigors of climate change, including floods, fires, droughts, high winds, and pests.*

A recent example is the survival of the famous banyan tree in Lahaina, Maui. The devastating wildfire that struck Lahaina in 2023 completely burned down the town and was so hot that it melted metal, and yet the town's 150-year-old banyan tree made it through and will survive. The redwoods in California's Big Basin Redwoods State Park have also proven unexpectedly resilient. After lightning fires in 2020 torched the canopy, it looked like most of the trees were going to die. But researcher Drew M. P. Peltier and others, in an article published in the scientific journal *Nature Plants*, observed that, instead, the trees used stored sugars to nourish buds that had been under their bark for centuries. Fresh growth sprouted from the blackened trunks!

Eventually, with the help of his sons, Jared and Jake, David managed to found Archangel Ancient Tree Archive. Jared was a director of AATA and board chair, and Jake helped figure out how to clone the old trees. Fortunately, when fires burned some of the precious ancient sequoias in California, they already had their clones. It is some

---

*See Pennisi, "Rare and Ancient Trees Are Key to a Healthy Forest"; and Robbins, "The Genetic Power of Ancient Trees."

comfort to know that trees with their hardy genetics have at least been replanted.

With redwoods, he takes cuttings from the sun needles found at the top of the over three-hundred-foot trees. Although David never shared what the archangels told him about meeting up with me, he did invite me to join him and his various teams whenever they came to Humboldt and Del Norte Counties to take clones or to be filmed. Once David's climbing crew even took me to the top of one of the redwoods. It was quite a climb.

Twice I had mentioned to David that I would love to go up in the canopy. Then David did something I thought would never actually happen: he invited me to ascend a redwood giant. Why had I told David that I wanted to go up? I most certainly did not! It was too scary. I'm afraid of heights. Terrified, I spent the next few weeks thinking of ways to get out of it. My mind spun excuses. Maybe I could say that my tummy hurt—which it certainly did from the stress of even thinking about going up a giant redwood two or three hundred feet into the sky. Or I could use my sore shoulder as an excuse.

But I'd look like a hypocrite if I didn't climb. Soon enough I found myself strapped into a harness and guided up the tree with AATA's climbing crew. At the top, I was greeted by a professional climber swinging blithely in his harness. He told me I could swing too, but I declined his generous offer. Instead, I trembled and clutched a branch with one hand, wrapped the other arm around the thin trunk at the top, and kept my feet securely on the limb below. The wind whispered through the fern fronds growing in tree cavities and rocked the tree gently. I felt like an eagle roosting high in her aerie, and some slight change came over my being.

The professional climber swung around the top of the tree like a monkey while I continued to grip the branch so hard that my knuckles turned numb and white. Peering over the canopy, I looked down on a lush fern mat, tufts of verdant green epiphytes that hang from crotches between branches in the trees. Leather-leaf ferns (*Polypodium scouleri*) are nourished by the loamy humus soil from decomposed bark and leaves that settles into these cavities. The soil can remain there undisturbed for hundreds of years. The ferns together with this soil form fern mats that can grow to be eight feet wide. Holding an astonishing amount of water—up to five thousand gallons per acre—the fern mats become a source of water for the redwoods, who grow aerial roots from their crowns right into the succulent mats so that they can suck the water up a relatively short distance instead of all the way from the ground. Insects and wandering salamanders (*Aneides vagrans*) are also nourished in the moist environment.

From my perch, I noticed a wandering salamander. I'd read that they feed on small, almost invisible bugs in the fern mats and may never even touch the ground. It was a heady feeling for me, quivering up at the top of the tree, imagining these creatures who never spend time on the ground—a complete lifetime in the sky.

I looked at the bright green tips of the sun needles that David and his team use to clone. Once they've taken the cuttings, Archangel Ancient Tree Archive gets them to their nursery as fast as possible and puts them in a hydroponic cloning solution. When the little trees are big enough, they are then shipped to hospitable places to grow around the world. They have planted champion tree clones in the states of Oregon, Washington, and California and in New Zealand, Ireland, Germany, and many more countries, where the ancient tree genetics now survive in Living Tree Libraries.

When I came down again, I knew I'd never be quite the same. "That was mind-blowing!" I told David. "It felt so different being up there, touching the sky."

David smiled. "Redwood trees act like antennas, bringing in the energies from all sorts of dimensions. Different frequencies of energy are received by different glands. What the pituitary is tuned into differs from what can be picked up by the adrenals."

I nodded, thinking that, whether from the base or the crown, we have only begun our exploration of consciously communing with trees. Our human survival and that of the trees is twined together as intimately as my body hugging the redwood.

I thought I'd never go up another tree again. Once was enough. But, then, while my husband, Steve, and I were in Sarasota, Florida, we met up again with David and some of his climbing crew, and I was invited up to the top of a magnificent old oak tree. I would have wriggled out of it, but another woman, Linda, had gone before me, and I somewhat stupidly thought, "If she can do it, so can I. How hard can it be?" I mean, after all, I'd done it once before in a much taller redwood.

Getting up wasn't too bad as they used the ropes to haul me up in what is known as an "elevator climb." At the top, I looked down on the subtropical plants of Florida, admiring the satiny green leaves of broad-leafed philodendrons and the waving tops of palm trees. Although I still clutched branches as if my life depended upon it, there was a heady joy in being up so high, on top of the world.

That was until one of the climbers told me the bad news. From his comfortable spot on a nearby branch, the professional climber said, "You have to step off into midair to get down."

I looked at the ground. My knees started to shake. "That's the only way?"

He nodded.

My hands clenched the rope so hard my fingers hurt.

"You can do it," the climber encouraged kindly.

"Maybe I need helicopter rescue," I said, only half-joking.

He smiled and directed: "First hold onto the rope and stand up straight."

I did as he said, my body quaking.

"When you're ready, move off the branch."

I willed myself to take that one small step into pure space. Instead, I screamed. Loudly.

Everyone on the ground looked up. Linda had made rappelling down from the tree look so easy. Now here I was, stuck.

Linda stood beneath the tree and called up, "Just step out."

I couldn't do it. Staring for a long time at a wispy white cloud while everyone waited for me to step off the branch, I watched the cloud shape itself into angel wings. Thinking, "Angels in the clouds, angels in the trees," I felt oddly comforted and protected. Taking a deep breath, I finally stepped off the branch. Sliding down the rope, I made my exhilarating way to the ground.

"That was so much fun!" I exclaimed, hugging everyone joyfully. "Thank you for getting me up there."

I felt lighter, freer, and clearer.

David asked, "What healing did you receive from the tree?"

I said something about feeling the beauty and shelter of the oak. Later, I realized that the real healing I'd received was the release of fear when I screamed. It wasn't only the fear of heights I'd let go of, it was also some of the fear that keeps me living small so I don't have to push my edges and feel it. Once again, my friends at Archangel Ancient Tree Archive helped me grow. They are very good at growing things!

Forest Guidance

If you would like to experience the forest canopy, research "Forest Canopy Walks." There are places, including Eureka, California, where aerial suspension bridges are available to the public to go up into the canopy. It does feel different up there, and if you get a chance to go to the leafy heights, you may want to compare the experience of that with the way you feel sitting on the ground. Personally, I feel more comfortable down on the ground! Like cats, circling around until they find their comfortable spot to lounge and purr, our bodies instinctively know where there is healing energy or kami. When you are settled, take in a few deep breaths. As you tune in more deeply, notice where you need a little more energy. It could be an organ, gland, muscle, or your big toe. Breathe into this area. Perhaps place your hands on it. Mentally ask the tree or other nature ally you are working with if she or he would like to help with your healing. For me, yes feels like a warmth in my belly, a sweetness in my heart, and a sense of expansion. On the other hand, no feels like a contraction, a tightening and shutting down. If the answer feels like a yes, open to receive. Afterward, give thanks and make an offering. This can be your gratitude, a song, prayer, or stone, water you infuse with blessing, or whatever feels right to you.

5
The Green Jewel

I am once again off to the woods. I seek the golden mead,
the honey nectar of a soul at peace.

The roots of my growth and healing from the trees took off long before I began forest bathing. Way back in 1987, while listening to a guided hypnotic meditation in an attempt to find my soul career, a green jewel was put into my throat and I was told I was to "speak for Earth."* At the time I had no idea what that could mean. I had recently given birth to my first daughter and couldn't picture myself heading off on some lecture circuit to talk about environmental issues.

Setting aside the vision with a sigh, I went back to diapers and giving piano lessons. Later, when I wrote a few articles and an environmental picture book, I thought, "Maybe this is it! Maybe I speak for Earth through writing." But no one wanted to publish that book, although I did sell a humorous picture book, *Princess Justina Albertina*, and a young adult dystopian novel, *Stolen Voices*. So I sighed again and went back to cooking, chauffeuring my kids to lessons, teaching a bit of creative writing, and giving piano lessons.

A couple years ago, thirty-three years later, I began to understand

---

*I listened to Orin's "Discovering Your Life Purpose" by Sanaya Roman, who channels guidance from Orin, a nonphysical being and spirit teacher.

what that meditation meant. Sitting with Grandmother Dragon Tree, I felt a sudden urge to allow the tree to speak through me. It happened over and over again.

Every time I tuned into Grandmother Dragon Tree, that same feeling of needing to speak for the tree arose. It felt like a pressure in my throat, like a frog wanting to leap out. But I had absolutely no idea how I was supposed to speak for a tree. Instead, I went back to the forest and enjoyed the creative exuberance of nature. I could almost perceive the nature spirits playing with the elements to create life in budding leaves and bursting blooms. I could almost hear the happy chatter of the fairies in my ears, almost see them dancing about, flitting from a huckleberry bush to a maple tree.

Often I went to Summer Tree. She first called me years ago. I was on an ordinary hike with my friend Annette. To reach Summer Tree, Annette and I drove fifty minutes. We passed a large lagoon with its long sand spit separating the smooth blue water from the crashing surf of the ocean. On the other side of the freeway, forested slopes rose in dense green foliage. When we reached the parking lot, we hiked along a flat trail for nearly four miles. After about a mile and a half, we crossed a large creek. During the rainy season, this creek can become a rapid river that is impossible to ford. Since we could only reach the tree during the summer, Annette and I called her Summer Tree.

Along the path, we greeted three absolutely giant redwoods that were probably over two thousand years old. We passed through groves of alder trees with green leaves shimmering in the breeze and watched two herons glide and skim the silky surface water of the creek.

Eventually, we came to a tree that looked so inviting, with her fallen needles forming a flat cushion for ten feet in front of her, that we couldn't resist sitting down. It was a perfect place to eat lunch. "This tree has almost the same diameter as that fallen log we passed with the plaque that says it is 750 years old," I observed. I knew that although the diameter of a tree can be one factor indicating age, it is not defini-tive. Tree trunks expand in size much more rapidly during wet years than when it's dry. That's why core samples revealing tree rings are more accurate. But it is invasive and potentially harmful to the tree, since the core samples are taken by using a pencil-sized drill to make a hole all the way to the center of the tree. This is a potential entryway for unwelcome insects, fungi, or other pests. Another method to guess the tree's age includes the way the canopy branches grow. Older trees tend to have interesting and oddly contorted shapes in their upper branches because they've survived all sorts of events: falling neigh-boring trees crashing into them and knocking off branches, lightning strikes and storms, times when the light was blocked by another tree and their limbs shot off in another direction seeking sun. Peering up into the treetop, I added, "This may not be the oldest tree in the for-est, but she sure is stunning."

Annette nodded, and we both admired Summer Tree's tall, straight trunk punctuated by a big burl one hundred feet up. The setting was incredible, with other giant redwoods nearby, as well as a clear view of the creek. The sound of water rippling over pebbles soothed us.

After we finished our lunches, Annette said, "Maybe we should try meditating here?" Annette has hosted many Tibetan Buddhist retreats on her property where we have both practiced meditating. Although I'd never meditated with a tree before, I replied, "Sure."

We shut our eyes and began focusing on our breath.

Forty minutes later, when I was deep into a wide open, spacious state of consciousness, a creaky voice spoke in my head, "Come back." Looking around, it was clear that no one had spoken. Annette's eyes were still closed and she was breathing softly, and there wasn't anyone else around. I shut my eyes again, and the voice repeated, "Come back. Sit . . . with me."

As soon as Annette and I opened our eyes, I told her, "I think the tree asked me to come back!"

On the return hike, we marveled. "Is it even possible for a tree to talk in your head?" asked Annette.

"I don't know!" I replied, "It seems crazy, but Grandmother Dragon Tree is still coming to me in my dreams."

Annette nodded. We often share our dreams with each other and have been in numerous dream retreats, where we have embodied the various animals and objects from our dreams.*

"I'm certainly going to visit this tree again," I said.

At the time, I thought maybe I'd return once or twice to Summer Tree to find out why I thought I'd heard her voice in my head. I had no idea that this was the beginning of a love affair with a tree that has lasted over fifteen years and continues to this day.

This was also the beginning of my hiking alone. In the past, I'd felt too scared to do so, but the next week when I wanted to return to Summer Tree, no one would go with me. I couldn't wait to get back to the tree, so I risked going alone. It turned out that, although at times I felt nervous, I liked being in the woods by myself. I felt more tuned into the environment, more present, and more aware than when I was with someone else.

Over the years, meditating with Summer Tree, and several other trees that I will introduce later in this story, that same urge to allow the trees to speak through me arose over and over again. It wasn't exclusively words that wanted to come through but more of a transmission. I felt kind of frustrated receiving this urge while in the presence of various trees because I still had no idea how I was supposed to do it. People would think I was nuts!

Then, out of nowhere, I began to receive invitations to share my forest-bathing experiences. First, Humanity Rising invited me to chan-

---

*Between 2012 and 2018 I attended five dream retreats in Bayside, California, with Susan Harper of Living Dreams Retreats. Embodying various animals and objects from our dreams helped reveal the existential truths our psyches were trying to communicate to us.

nel from the trees. I did so for about six minutes, although I don't remember exactly what came through because I was in an almost hypnagogic state and remembering is like pulling back the wisp of a dream. That was followed by a few more podcast hosts and interviewers asking me to share wisdom from the trees.

Clearly, something larger than me was going on here. I rose to the occasions as best I could, remembering that I'd vowed to the trees that I'd serve them. Whenever I allowed the trees to speak through me, there was a satisfied "mission accomplished" sort of feeling. When I returned to the trees, I felt a celebratory atmosphere, as if they were happy with me. Even my friend Allegra felt it. "The trees are happy with you today," she said.

How did she know? How could we tell the trees were happy? I felt it too, a sort of happy atmosphere. We wondered if any of this was real.

We do know that trees affect our mental, spiritual, and physical well-being, but as yet we have no proof that trees are aware of us. It's not impossible, however, considering that scientists have been showing that trees are sentient beings that communicate with one another through a network of fungi in the soil. They ask for and receive various nutrients like nitrogen, carbon, and water. They can even tell one another when to defend against insects and other pests. A Douglas fir attacked by insects may send chemical messengers to a nearby ponderosa pine, and then the pine tree will make enzymes to defend against the insects. The trees communicate information.

My intuitive sense is that the trees are conscious and aware beings and that they somehow know that I have done what they asked and allowed them to speak through me. They've been on the planet so much longer than we have. What is this tree picking up from my skin gently touching her bark?

I'm living in the realm of the mystical, exploring the borders of human potential and interspecies communication, using the fine-tuned instrument of my body to perceive through my five senses and the more subtle senses of intuition, insight, and instinct. My gut tells me there is something vast going on here. We inhabit a mystery. Science is my bedrock, letting me know what we know we know—and then there are the flights of fancy that soar me into the possible.

Some of those flights have proven true. One time, sitting with Winter Tree, I smelled smoke. There were no fires on the West Coast of the United States, and so I speculated about what it could be. As I dove deeper into the stillness of my meditation, a voice in my head that I imagined was the tree, since it was slow and didn't sound like my usual thoughts, said, "The smoke is from fires in Siberia."

I hadn't heard or read a thing about any fires in Siberia but went home and googled. Sure enough, there were fires in Siberia and articles saying that they were so huge that the smoke from them had reached all the way to the West Coast of the United States!

How did the trees know? Or how did they connect me to whatever intelligence did know?

Sitting in the knowing I do not know, I allow myself to relax into the beauty I do know. It's spring, and everything is glorious. Water in the creeks is crystal clear. Even after heavy rains, the water in an old-growth redwood forest usually remains clear because the plants and their roots absorb and filter the water, preventing soil runoff. We don't have to have muddy brown rivers taking the precious topsoil we need to grow food, plants, and trees out to sea, leaving a beige line hundreds of feet off shore.

There is so much we can learn from the remaining intact environments. Nature weaves each strand together in a sophisticated system where every element and life-form is essential and in balance and contributes to the whole. People are beginning to copy this with edible food forest gardens. Forest gardens mimic nature and require very little work once they are established because they use native plants and trees. Tall trees are planted with a layer of shrubs in front of them, followed by herbs, root crops, and vines. The trick is to think about how each species of plant interacts with the others so that the whole system works together.

Coral reef restoration is another area where people are learning from nature. Coral reefs bleach when warmer ocean waters kill the algae the coral feed upon. To help the coral survive, scientists are experimenting with breeding some of the more heat-resistant kinds of algae. Another example of copying the balance found in nature, the NGO Coral Guardian has successfully transformed the dead bleached-white reefs around Hatamin Island, east of Australia, into a vibrant and colorful oasis of life. Part of how they do this is by planting nursery-grown corals back onto the reefs. The musical sounds fish make may also help to bring coral reefs back to life. Cusk eels and other fish strum their swim bladders like drums, most likely to attract mates to spawn. A healthy coral reef is full of the calls of whales, fish, and even snapping shrimp. Dead coral reefs are eerily silent. Marine biologist Aran Mooney at the Woods Hole Oceanographic Institution in Massachusetts is collaborating with other scientists to see if putting recordings of fish sounds by dead coral reefs will help them to be restored. The sounds of fish singing attract small animals that look like tiny jellyfish to attach and hopefully encourage more fish to return to the recovering coral reef.*

Feeling heartened by these successful attempts at environmental restoration, I am once again off to the woods. I seek the golden mead, the honey nectar of a soul at peace. I seek this in cascading creeks, in bubbling springs, in the silence and stillness that allows me to come home to myself. I seek without expecting to find, and yet, again and again, I do find medicine, the waters of life that nourish.

---

*See Aizenman, "Fish Make Music!"; and Wetzel, "Bizarre Fish Songs Raise Hope for Coral Reef Recovery."

Forest Guidance

Blue spaces have similar powerful healing effects to being in forests. Time by rivers, oceans, lakes, waterfalls, and even fountains is shown to boost mood, lower stress, and increase health and well-being.* I think being in any place in nature has healing benefits. Do you have access to a park, tree, beach, desert, mountain, rainforest, or river? How about a backyard or even window garden? You are invited to find somewhere where you can be in contact with nature. I've found that it is possible to cultivate relationships with flora and fauna the same way we do with beloved friends and family. When we return again and again to the same places in all seasons and weathers, we notice subtle changes. We know where to find the ripe thimble berries, or catch the salmon swimming upstream to spawn. What place is beckoning to you?

---

*See Hunt, "Blue Spaces"; and Hicks, "Treating the Blues."

6
Redwoods and Whales

We are the soft hairs on Earth's body, caressing the
atmosphere, receiving intelligence from stars.

Steve and I promised ourselves a family trip to Hawaii after he made it through some medical treatments. It was something to dream about when things got challenging. Then COVID-19 struck, and we couldn't go anywhere. I kind of liked the forced retreat of the pandemic years. Finally, in a society that has selected for the social, go-go-go personality of extroverts, the skills I'd developed as an introvert were valuable; I was endlessly self-entertaining and happy with my own company. Life slowed down, and about all I did was walk on the beach or in the forest, read, play piano, cook, eat too much, meditate, do easy restorative yoga, talk on the phone, write, and try to paint. Dropping all social obligations felt like a relief. My life became spacious and easy, although I was aware of the extreme suffering endured by people who did not have the luxury of being retired, especially the essential workers who were most at risk. One of my daughters is a high school teacher with a young child, and the pandemic made life insanely stressful for her and her students. My more extroverted friends, especially the musicians, missed being able to get together. I still dreamed of snorkeling tropical seas.

We finally had the chance to realize our dream in the winter of

2022 when we met our two daughters, their partners, and our two-and-a-half-year-old granddaughter in Maui. Right after we left, there was a 6.4 earthquake in Humboldt County. Some buildings were reduced to rubble, and friends told us the shaking lasted so long that they were traumatized. That was the beginning. While we were gone, California was slammed by storm after storm, with high winds blowing trees down on decks, houses, and cars. Power outages were common. Allegra told me she couldn't make it down her driveway for a couple of days because live power poles were down, and PG&E, the utility company that provides gas and electric to Northern and Central California, was so swamped with similar emergencies all over the county that it couldn't get to her house immediately, as it would usually do.

Watching the disasters in California unfold from Maui was surreal. We couldn't believe how fortunate we were in missing such a harsh winter, and we worried for our friends, worried the huge old pine outside our house would topple onto the roof. But there was nothing we could do. We couldn't even get home when we planned because flights were canceled due to the inclement weather, and so we pulled out our credit cards and stayed two more unaffordable but blissful weeks, swimming in turquoise seas with whale songs all around.

Floating. Sounds. Long. Slow. Various pitches. High. Low. Singing tranquility, wrapping me in a rocking moving lullaby. I am held in whale songs. Every day, for over five weeks, when I snorkel amid the green sea turtles, marveling at bright-yellow and purple fish, I am held by these beautiful rounded tones. The notes calm me, entice me, and make me curious about their meaning. It is like listening to a foreign language I've studied a little bit. I can almost understand.

Somehow the whales seem to imbibe starlight, sending cosmic energy out in their love songs, informing the sea of an ancient knowing that feels familiar and far away, all at once. Opening myself more, I imagine the lighted song lines crossing oceans and gently being received by the land.

Whales are calling us, if we can understand.

The trees are also calling us.

While I'm in Maui, Ancestor Tree calls me in a dream all the way from the redwoods of California. In the dreamscape, I am walking deep into the redwood forest when I come to her unmistakable gnarled trunk. She has so many burls. They are knobby and rough protrusions. Usually burls on the trunk grow after the tree has been injured from fungal infestations, parasitic mistletoe, or insects. The tree reacts by creating a big bump that can come in all sorts of shapes and sizes. I think of it as similar to the way our skin forms scabs over injuries, although scabs eventually go away and burls do not. They add lots of character to the old redwoods, and it's easy to see all sorts of figures and faces in the burls.

In the dream, I walk up to the tree and stand next to one of the burls a few feet up the trunk. It looks like a dragon, with one unblinking eye staring back at me. The dragon's eye glows with golden light! I feel the tree beckoning me. She wordlessly conveys the thought that she wants me to come visit and bring the whale songs back to her.

It's astonishing to be called by a tree in a dream. I know I'm not the only one who has had this experience. In her book *Thus Spoke the Plant*, Monica Gagliano describes being called from Australia all the way to Peru by a tropical tree known as Socoba. Socoba also informs an Amazonian shaman that she has called Monica in her dreams to come work with her. Together with the shaman, Monica opens to plant-teacher-human conversation and learns that Socoba can heal our emotional, spiritual, and physical bodies.

Waking from my Ancestor Tree dream, the impulse to return and visit this ancient being deep in the heart of the forest and bring the whale songs to her pulses within me. The impulse feels like it is coming from outside myself, from the tree. Somehow I know that I am supposed to bring Allegra with me. I'm not surprised. Both of us marvel at how much more magical we are together than individually. We've nicknamed ourselves "the dynamic duo" and often theorize that the reason there is so much potent energy when we are outside together is because I tend to bring in the elemental energies and the angels tag along with Allegra. When the elementals and angels get together with us in our human hearts, it's so lively that we are challenged to hold on to our seats.

Once Steve and I finally do make it home from Hawaii, the storms are still so ferocious that it's too dangerous to hike in the redwoods where branches continue to break off and fall. Instead, I visit the more open forest of the Sitka spruce trees on the cliffs by the sea. Even there, scores of trees came down. I'm filled with the poignant feeling I might have upon seeing a beloved friend or family member who went through something hard when I wasn't there to be with them. I'm equally aware that had I stayed, I would have just huddled in my house with the power going on and off, worried about trees smashing into the roof.

After a couple of weeks at home, the day finally comes when Allegra and I hike through the ferns and freshly hydrated forest to Ancestor Tree. Branches, debris and some fallen trees are scattered everywhere. Despite that, the forest is deeply quiet and peaceful, full of powerful energy. It's tangible, like some sort of life-giving plasma, a clear diamond-like substance. This forest has been left mostly alone, with few human visitors this winter. The particles in the air feel alive and nourishing. The pure essence has built up into a palpable nectar of life. We inhale the fresh crisp air, cool on our skin, and smell resins from fallen fronds. There's magic in the air.

And then it happens. We reach Ancestor Tree, and I sense the whale energy meet the redwoods, alive and anchoring from my field into this holy spot at her base. Feeling the flowing element of water—absorbent, flexible, impressionable—Allegra and I spontaneously dance a clumsy hula, but in our minds' eyes we see a beautiful young Hawaiian woman, shiny black hair to her waist, dancing the hula so gracefully in her ocean blue dress that she looks like a sea goddess undulating with the waves.

Allegra and I sing, and it feels like the whales are sending love and support to this forest, battered from storms so ferocious they've been named bomb cyclones. Green tendrils wrap around the melodies, earth and sea coming together in harmony, whales and redwoods sharing their tending and revitalizing care for the lines of light and song, of love and connectivity that circle Earth: Gaia's net of aware intelligence. I can almost taste a time long ago, perhaps in my ancestral memory or in my imagination, when I could understand the songs of whales and birds, the croaks of frogs, and the full exquisite symphony of life.

As I sing the song of the whales, I realize it was thirteen years ago that I wrote a memoir I never planned to publish, "Singing with Whales." In the story, I predicted a time when I'd be fully healed and find myself singing with whales. At the time of writing, I was overwhelmed raising my daughters, not sleeping well, and suffering from fibromyalgia and chronic fatigue. Tears of gratitude well up in my eyes when I realize that time of feeling healed has finally come.

Immersion in wild beauty has been the main ingredient in the tonic that has healed me. It is the mythical holy wellspring. Earth loves us. She keeps us alive. We are the soft hairs on Earth's body, caressing the atmosphere, receiving intelligence from stars.

Forest Guidance

Go to or imagine you are in a beautiful setting. Allow your inner awareness to guide you, as I did when I was doing the dance of the whales. Alternate walking with sitting or lying down. Walk by lifting one leg to an in-breath and then lift the other leg on an outbreath. This is Zen master Thich Nhat Hanh's walking meditation and is a very slow movement, which helps us to slow down, allowing for a feeling of more spaciousness.* Repeat until you feel you are in an altered state of consciousness. (Note to hikers: When I'm hiking, this practice is a little too slow to get anywhere, so I often vary it by breathing in for four steps and then out for the next four. Even though I'm moving quickly along the path, this practice brings me into more awareness and fluid motion. It is, however, not the same practice because it misses that important element of slowing down.) As we slow down, it becomes possible to feel into subtle proprioceptive movement. Follow these inner currents that flow through your body until you find sensations that originate from deep within and allow those sensations to move you. For example, instead of moving your hand, allow your hand to lead the movement, which may be very small. Pretend you are a tree, rooted and reaching to the sky. Sway in the wind. Imagine you are drinking in starlight, and it is filling you with sweetness.

---

*I learned this meditation from Cynthia Jurs who received the Dharmacharya transmission to teach from Thich Nhat Hanh in 1994. I have taken online meditation classes from her from 2019 to the present.

7

Obstacles along the Path

That seems like the edge we need to walk now—being aware of what is happening, allowing our hearts to stay open to grief, and yet not missing the miracle of our lives.

February at home, and it is still storming almost every day, sometimes even hailing and snowing, which almost never happens here on the coast. I love being out in storms. The elementals are so alive and active then. There's an exuberant joy, an exultant power, in the fresh scent of moistened earth and bark and the creaking, groaning, rattling sounds of branches swaying in wind.

One day, it's cloudy but not stormy, so Steve and I go to the redwoods. I need to connect with the ancient trees because I've been invited to an interview about forest bathing with Justine Toms of New Dimensions Radio. I want to be infused with the energy of redwoods so that I can share this enchanting environment with people.

Picking a less-popular trail, Steve and I hike into the hush of the woods. This time of year, the songbirds aren't back, and the quiet is barely broken by the occasional caw of a crow. Caw, caw, caw. As if the crow is greeting us. A small creek babbles nearby, splashing and plashing. It's wonderful to see streams full of water again after the long drought. Plants are plumped up. Brilliant green moss grows like velvet on boulders and logs. I can't resist gently running my hand over the squashy surface.

Spiderwebs crisscross the trail, a sure sign no one has been out here lately. We head up the path. Even after all this rain, there is very little mud. Old forests absorb water like sponges: plants, trees, roots, all drinking in moisture. But the roots along the trail are wet and slippery, so I use my poles and step carefully.

Trees tower above us. Redwood trees have cones and are therefore conifers along with pine, spruce, and cedar trees. Conifers have been around for hundreds of millions of years, surviving disasters like the meteors that made dinosaurs go extinct.

Walking through the forest, I notice trees so wide that it would take eight of us with arms outstretched holding hands to circle one of them. It feels great in here, like I'm in a temple or cathedral, certainly a holy place. My being effortlessly goes into a state of reverence. I'm in awe. And utterly grateful to feel like this. Immersing myself in the forest has taken me out of myself, out of my worries and concerns, out of my busy mind with the endless to-do lists. There is nowhere I'd rather be right now, nothing else I'd rather be doing. I'm here! It feels like a blessing.

Then we come upon a fallen rhododendron tree. It's a bit of a scramble, stepping over protruding branches without getting impaled, but Steve and I manage and continue on our way up the trail, listening to the drip, drip of droplets falling from the canopy. We walk free for another quarter mile until we come upon the next obstacle, another fallen rhododendron. This time, we have to crawl under the tree to get through. It's not too bad, and I notice how fresh and loamy the watered soil smells. There's a banana slug glopping along at eye level as I crawl and a millipede. I am careful not to touch the yellow-spotted millipede; when they sense danger this invertebrate has been known to contract into a ball and release hydrogen cyanide, a toxic chemical that smells a bit like almonds. It probably wouldn't harm me, but I don't want to find out with a skin rash.

Marveling at my new close-to-the-ground perspective, I make my way through the tangled l leaves until I can stand again. "I wonder how many trees are down," I ask Steve.

"Hopefully not too many more," he replies, and then we sink back into reverent silence. The next fallen tree is a Douglas fir that took down a nearby California bay laurel. I'm noticing that lots of trees toppled others as they fell. Some are leaning precariously against their neighbors. Will this make the neighboring trees more vulnerable in the next storm?

The forest is a mess, and I'm literally wriggling on my belly to get through. This is not exactly what I had in mind for my hike today. My clothes are dirty, and I've tweaked my shoulder from twisting myself to dodge a branch. A twig poked my eye, and leaves have scraped my face. We're already halfway on a loop trail though, so there's not much point in turning around.

A budding trillium, the precious white flower not yet unfurled, is at eye level. I pause and take a breath. Even though there are obstacles along my path, it is still beautiful. It's like life, I think, questioning if there is a teaching for me here. Even though I'm uncomfortably on my belly, is it possible for me to stop and appreciate this one small flower?

How can I slither through the debris, grieving fallen trees, knowing that this year there will be fewer rhododendrons arching my trails in glorious pink, and at the same time love the display of life renewing itself that is this one blooming trillium?

That seems like the edge we need to walk now—being aware of what is happening, allowing our hearts to stay open to grief, and yet not missing the miracle of our lives. I get up again for another easy stretch of trail, knowing that we face many obstacles, but the flowers are still blooming and they are worth our attention.

Forest Guidance

Where are the obstacles in your life? Even in the midst of these challenges, what are you grateful for? Paying attention to the beauty of varied landscapes and seascapes evokes states of awe, reverence, joy, and appreciation. According to an article by clinical psychologist Madhuleena R. Chowdhury, these feelings help us heal. This has certainly been accurate for me. When I began forest bathing, I had no idea that being so excited about going to the forest and then spending time marveling at how gorgeous it was would have such a profound effect upon my state of being, but it has. I began to live in an eager state of joy, with that "can't wait" for something good to happen feeling I remembered from childhood before my birthday. This sort of joie de vivre gave me a lot more vitality, and I began to heal from my chronic health problems. What makes you feel awe, reverence, and joy? Is there a place in nature that uplifts and enlivens you or makes you feel grateful that so much beauty exists? If you can, go there and share your gratitude with nature. Notice how you feel afterward. If you do not already have such a place available, go there in your imagination, watch a nature channel on TV, buy a potted orchid, or look at artwork portraying scenes from the natural world. Spending as much time as we can focusing on what we love is healing.

8
Holy Groves

Inaudible laughter sparkles in my ears, and I feel
so much elemental joy that I'm leaping across logs,
gamboling about the woods, prancing with
the fairies in capering glee.

April. Finally a warm day. Peeling sweater and jacket, I wear a
T-shirt and balmy air touches my bare skin. Steve and I walk
down into a holy grove of very ancient redwoods, some probably over
two thousand years old. On the way down, we notice many California
bay laurel trees have fallen. Trail crews have cleared them to the side,
but the forest is full of tumbled trees. In the grove, a huge redwood
fell. Inhaling the resins, I remind myself that this tree is still part of
the forest. As the coastal redwood rots, a process that can take hundreds of years, she will provide homes for moss, ferns, lichen, bugs, and
beetles of all sorts. Fungi grow out of the fallen trunk. Shelf mushrooms, like the ruffled and striated copper-golden-beige turkey tail I'm
seeing, are saprotophs. Saprotrophs nourish themselves by decompos-
ing organic matter and recycling nutrients back into the soil.

Some bigleaf maples have been halved, half the tree gone. My heart
sinks to see them so diminished. They have so much character, leaves
dancing against the blue sky; their twisting thick branches ending
abruptly in short stubby fingers, as if they are making hand gestures.

Continuing around the grove, I am happy to see how full and healthy the creek looks for the first time in years. Maybe there will be more otters this year. I used to see them frolicking in the water all the time, but these past few drought years, I've rarely come across river otters. I miss having them around more often. It's always such a happy feeling to see wildlife, a sense of not being alone on Earth. A couple of ducks fly by, and I take a side trail down to the water.

Wading in the rapidly flowing water, I'm tempted to plunge into the safer backwater eddy for that first baptismal dip of spring. That initial watery immersion always makes me feel washed clean, tingling with vibrancy and life force energy. I want to do it. The sand is hot. Telling myself that I will be able to warm up again, I wade in up to my knees. Standing there for a long while, I try to get my courage up to at least dunk, but my feet are crimson red, my knees are numb. It's freezing. April is too soon for me; I will try again in May.

Back up in the grove, I continue circling. The trees here feel like they know one another well, companions standing together in a circle for centuries. Most of the redwoods made it through the storms and are still standing tall.

Settling myself close to Star Tree, I relax in the welcome shade. Usually it is so cool in the redwood forest that I'm only warm in the sun, but today is around eighty degrees. Closing my eyes, I allow myself to let go of my chronically busy mind. At first, I notice a band of pressure around my skull. Breathing into that band, it loosens up. Then I focus on my heart, and the sweet sensation of love blossoms like the redwood violets all around. Old-timers used to make vinegar, tea, and even candy out of these violets, which are related to pansies, but there aren't as many of them around to harvest any more, and most of those are in protected parks, where we are fortunately not allowed to pick anything. I can never get over the fact that they are called violet when they are most definitely yellow. For a long time, I argued with my friend Annette, "These can't be violets. They are yellow!" She insisted they were, and finally I looked it up and reluctantly admitted she was right.

See how my thoughts drift in meditation? It's like trying to tame a feral beast. I give up and focus on my breath, watching one thought after another roll past like clouds, aware that sky mind is always present underneath the clouds. Eventually, even though I can count the times on one hand when I'm not thinking anything and focused on my breath, my thoughts do slow down, and I experience a more capacious state. It's easier out here. There is space all around: sky, trees, earth, river, and the rocky gravel bar. It's quiet. I'm not bombarded with electricity, microwaves, traffic sounds, radios, televisions, and all the noise of our towns and cities. No one is watching me. Opening up is innate, like a flower in the sun.

I know I have the opportunity for a moment of pure presence. Instead, I start thinking of this grove of trees and recall when I tended a grove of women as part of TreeSisters, a nonprofit UK charity founded by Clare Dubois that supports tree planting in tropical countries. At that time, TreeSisters invited women all over the world to become Grove Tenders, in an effort to restore women as well as forests. We were connected, grove to grove, in a forest floor of women. It was messy, alive, constantly changing, and in that forest mulch, many of us felt we grew by quantum leaps. Some women, including me, stepped up and said they'd like to be Grove Tenders. We gathered groups in circles and used a technique created by Clare known as sistering. Part of this technique, which can be practiced by men as well as women, includes taking turns gazing at each other, looking for the beauty in each person. It feels vulnerable to be seen this way, and the love often lowered our defenses so that we broke down in tears as old hurts released.

Many people have both personal and inherited trauma. There's a lot to heal. Circles where we feel safe and heard, where we listen to each other, perhaps passing a talking stick around, is a way to come back to what is true for each of us. Healing happens when we begin with the truth of how we really feel, where we honestly are right now, and allow both the joy and the pain to open our hearts. Pain felt and shared usually transforms, passing through us in purifying waves that leave us more energy to respond to what is happening now.

I miss my grove. First, I moved away to get medical care for my husband. Like much of rural America, Humboldt County has a serious doctor shortage. Many people can't get a doctor at all, and even when you do have a doctor, you still have to leave the area for most procedures requiring specialists. By the time we returned, the pandemic had us locked down, and it was too hard to gather inside. Now TreeSisters no longer includes groves.

I am surprised to realize how much I miss the sistering and other aspects of TreeSisters. As well as sistering, TreeSisters used to include founder Clare Dubois's Inner Journey around the "Map of Awakening." This map was given to her in a vision. We journeyed from reveal, embrace, embody, activate, and shine. In the center of the map, we found belonging. Kathleen Brigidina added "Liberating Our Creative Voices" to the TreeSisters' Inner Journey, and women were encouraged in the relationship between art and restoring ourselves and the environment.

So many of the problems we now face are human induced; to solve them at their roots and not re-create the big mess, we are going to have to heal ourselves, including everyone: men, women, and children, as well as our interspecies relationships. Sistering is a powerful healing tool. Chiding myself for all this thinking, I hope I'm going to actually meditate today at Star Tree. Reining in my totally out-of-control mind, I breathe and vow that I am going to relax here with Star Tree and go into a real meditation.

According to David Milarch of AATA, trees vibrate higher than human beings. Paradoxically, we have to slow down to connect with them. Eventually I do. I know I have when delicate currents of love stream into my heart, similar to the way I felt holding my newborn daughter. My pulse slows. My heart beat is steady. Swallowing, I taste the last bit of sour redwood sorrel I've been nibbling. Inhaling the moist earthy smell, I'm finally at long last all here. It feels good. It feels wide open. There's room to breathe and be, see and sense, hear and touch. My subtle senses awaken, too, and knowing creeps in.

Knowing, or *gnosis*, includes the sensation of Star Tree, standing tall, her trunk coursing with awareness from both ground and sky. I feel her majesty. Star Tree envelops me in her presence, embracing me in her energetic field. It feels almost as if she senses me as part of her. I know I sense her as part of me. It's deeply relaxing, this unfurling into being more than my boxed-in-the-body self. At the same time, I'm more aware of my body than usual. Like the tree's roots, I root deeply into my embodied experience. Like the tree's branches, I grow into the unified field. Nestling in, held in her presence, I know that trees do help us awaken. It's no accident Buddha was enlightened after meditating underneath the Bodhi Tree for forty-nine days. Being with trees calms our nervous systems.

To me, being with the old trees feels similar to when I received cranial sacral therapy, and the practitioner commented that she could feel the long tides in my body. She explained that the three main tides are the fluctuations of the circulating cerebral spinal fluid in the body and that it is possible to perceive them. Although the long tides are always with us, we are often too distracted to feel their slow pace. As she worked on me with this form of hands-on healing, I relaxed completely. This is similar to what I experience with trees. Gentle pulsations flow through my body, and I picture them like sap flowing through the heartwood of the tree. In those moments, I feel like the tree and I are kin.

From this place of open attention, the thoughts floating gently through my mind are not so fast. They are full of guidance, in tune with my gut knowing. A raven on a nearby branch stares at me with bright eyes that say the bird knows I've arrived, and so do I.

When we get here in the present moment, we may discover simplicity. We may also discover vast, delicate, interwoven complexity. The present moment includes more than the physical reality we can access through our five senses. The present moment is replete with subtle dimensions of reality. Limitless possibilities arise.

After a timeless time of sitting peacefully, I begin to sense the elementals all around me. They are brimming with joy and the creative vivacity of spring. They dart about, twirling, pirouetting, flitting through branches, skipping and dancing—blue, violet, white, pink, yellow, green. The fairies have come out to play. I get up and waltz around the forest, frolicking about with my not-quite-visible friends. Inaudible laughter sparkles in my ears, and I feel so much elemental joy that I'm leaping across logs, gamboling about the woods, prancing with the fairies in capering glee. "Wherever our feet touch the earth, new life arises," whispers my imaginary yellow fairy.

Spinning on my toes, I think-ask back, "For me, too?"

"Yes, silly," chortles the shimmering fairy. "Don't you know? You, too, are part of the dance of life."

Forest Guidance

Some of the women in the grove I tended felt too vulnerable at first to practice sistering, including myself. At first, I worried that maybe I was doing it wrong and not guiding the group correctly. But after being with Clare Dubois on a retreat in Mendocino County as well as participating in her online sistering offerings, I realized that it was the practice itself, and not how I was conveying it, that made us feel exposed. So, in the grove I tended, we tiptoed into sistering. One woman started by receiving the unconditionally loving gaze of her dog. I began by trying out the technique with Grandmother Dragon Tree. Gazing at the tree, it was easy to look for and find her beauty. Then I imagined the tree also perceiving me as beautiful. Whether or not the tree actually perceived me at all, imagining that she was appreciating me left me feeling open and relaxed. Another option we explored in our grove was to allow the person receiving loving attention to begin with her eyes closed. That way she could bask in the energy without that nervous feeling many of us experience when someone is staring at us, no matter how kindly. Eventually, we were able to practice sistering with our eyes open. Afterward, women said they felt lighter, clearer, and relieved of burdens they didn't even know they were carrying. If you'd like to try this yourself, check out Clare Dubois's YouTube videos for more detailed instructions: "Inner Journey Week Two Embrace: How to Trust Togetherness, with Clare Dubois" and "TreeSisters Groves: Sistering with Clare Dubois."

9
Eagles and Condors

To preserve and restore ourselves, we need to
preserve and restore the wild places,
which can be medicine for everyone.

Back down by the flowing water, lying in the hot sand, staring up at treetops brushing the blue sky, I see a large bird lazily circling above. It's too big to be a hawk, too dark to be an osprey, and doesn't look like one of the bald eagles I often see out here. Their heads are white. It's probably a turkey vulture, I think, squinting and wishing I'd brought binoculars. The feathers on the wing tips are separated like those of a turkey vulture, but the bird doesn't look quite like they do. Sitting up, I watch the bird fly closer. Glimpsing telltale patches of white under the wings, I point, "I think that's one of the condors the Yurok Tribe released!"

"It sure is soaring," Steve says, and we are both so excited by this sighting. Condors are an endangered species and were extinct in the wild in California until the local Yurok Tribe began freeing the birds out of captivity in 2022. Eight condors were released that year, with three more released the following year.* It's incredible how quickly birds who have lived in captivity their whole lives fly off into the sky.

---

*For information about the Yurok Condor Restoration Program, see the Yurok Tribe website.

Because condors do spend time on the ground, their predators include bears, bobcats, and mountain lions, but the birds are tagged and have been watched closely. So far so good. They've been thriving.

My heart warms that humans can restore condors to the wild. It seems so hopeful. I have heard various versions of an old indigenous prophecy from the Amazon about the eagle and the condor. They talk about human societies going in two different directions. People in North America following the eagle develop the intellect and a more industrial, masculine path, while those of the condor in South America follow the feminine path of heart. Condor people stay in touch with their intuition and live in harmony, so connected to Earth that they feel her pain as their own. There is a danger the people of the eagle, lacking in empathy, will dominate to the point of both harming Earth and driving the condor people to extinction.

Some versions of the prophecy say that once the eagle and condor fly together in the sky, there is a potential for a new era in human consciousness to arise. People from North and South America could unite with respect for diversity and deep connection to Earth, and it would be the beginning of an enormous healing. It reminds me of the indigenous prophecy shared by Robin Wall Kimmerer in *Braiding Sweetgrass*: there are two roads humanity may take, one that is grassy and green and the other that tears up our feet. A similar 1,200-year-old Tibetan Buddhist prophecy is found in Joanna Macy's book *World as Lover, World as Self*: a time of crisis will come when ordinary people rise up as Shambhala warriors who combine insight and compassion to create healing and change. Throughout *The Book of the Hopi*, Frank Waters shares the Hopi prophecy that the fourth world, which we are currently in, will end by violent weather. According to the Hopi, the first world was harmonious until it was destroyed by fire—probably volcanic eruptions or comets. The second world was destroyed by ice, and we have all heard of the Ice Age. The third world was destroyed by floods or one giant flood, which has been recorded in the Bible (Noah and the Ark) and many other stories and sacred texts. According to Hopi beliefs, the grand finales of these civilizations were not happenstance but rather due to humanity not following the spiritual laws of the Creator or living in right relationship with Earth. Our current fourth world is predicted to end from violent weather, and this is happening now. But, concurrently, we are birthing a fifth world that seeds in plants, the stars, and our human hearts. We are in the midst of old ways dying while at the same time birthing new ways of love and compassion. It's pretty bumpy, right? And all of the prophecies indicate that realizing the potential for our evolution into a more peaceful world depends upon the choices we make.

Some of the prophecies have been kept sacred and carefully tended over the past five hundred years by the Q'eros, descendants of the Incans, who live high in the Andes Mountains of Peru. Now the time has come when they are sharing these prophecies with us.* Surprisingly, about fifteen years ago, I found myself compelled to find someone qualified to transmit the nine rites of the Munay-Ki offered by the Q'ero to me. I discovered the Four Winds Society, founded by medical anthropologist Alberto Villoldo, who brought the rites to the West. The rites are energetic transmissions for Healer, Bands of Power, Harmony, Seer, Day Keeper, Wisdom Keeper, Earth Keeper, Star Keepers, and Creator. Actually, I lost interest after receiving Earth Keeper and have yet to receive the last two rites. I guess I haven't been ready to integrate them. Mother Earth has certainly been keeping me busy learning directly from her!

The condor and the eagle coming back together is a symbol that we are entering an era of new possibilities. If humanity learns to integrate the strength and intellect of the eagle with the compassion and peaceful ways of the condor, then we can live healthy lives for many

---

*See Spirit Maji, "The Prophecy of the Andes Q'eros: Eagle & Condor," SpiritMaji: God Is the Red Pill, 2023.

generations into the future. It is up to us how we respond to the pivotal times we are living within.

How can we respond when our hearts are broken, when we are shattered from unbearable personal and collective wounds? How can we heal when the air and water are polluted and make us sick? How can we heal when pesticides kill the pollinators we need? How can we heal when there are so many fires that the air is unhealthy and some people are forced to evacuate their homes? The alternative of not healing is unthinkable and certainly not writable for me, and so I think about how we can heal. Healing will have to happen in many ways all at once. For me, a big piece of the puzzle is nature connection. I've personally experienced the astonishing healing power of wilderness. Being out in pristine environments has brought me well-being, a deeper sense of myself, and joy at being alive. I want everyone to be able to experience the healing power of nature.

Watching the condor circle in the azure sky until the huge bird is a small speck, I swirl my toes into the warm sand. When I can no longer see the condor, I lie back down and close my eyes, feeling the sand contour to my body through the sarong I'm lying upon. It is comforting and reminds me of the way the cool, white sand beaches of Florida's Siesta Key felt. Except it wasn't quiet there. Here, I hear the sound of the river flowing by, an occasional whisper of wind through the trees, and a few peeping birds.

In Florida there were many people talking on the beach, and I recognized accents from all over the country: the short, clipped speech of New Yorkers, the slow drawl of Texans, the distinctive "oh, howdy" of the Midwest. I heard Cuban Spanish, Portuguese, a little French, and a bunch of languages I couldn't even recognize. It sounded like flocks of different birds chattering all around me. Opening my eyes, I also saw Amish women in long dresses and bonnets wading in the water close to young women in thong bikinis. A streak of gladness shot through my heart. It felt so celebratory, seeing people from different religious and cultural beliefs as well as many races and nationalities all enjoying a peaceful day at the beach together.

Before the civil rights movement of the 1950s and 1960s, legalized racist beliefs denied Black people the right to relax at most Florida beaches. It's hot in Florida! I can't imagine living there without being able to refresh myself in the water. Sadly, this summer of 2023, water at some of Florida's beaches was over 100 degrees and I doubt anyone was able to cool off.

A fresh draft gusts up the river canyon, and I'm pulled out of my Siesta Key reverie and back into my present time in the forest. I drifted off, probably because it feels so safe when Steve is here with me. Alone, I'm always on the lookout. Mostly I'm afraid of mountain lions. With two people, we make enough noise that lions seldom show themselves. But I'm also alert to the point of being hypervigilant when I come across a man on the trails. A frisson of fear shoots through me. Will he attack me? So far the men passing me on trails have been respectful, and I haven't had any problems. But the instinctual fear in a world where so many women are raped takes over. My heart beats faster and my palms sweat as I check out the fellow walking by. I feel grateful that I'm an "old lady" and not preyed upon the way young women are, although I'm also aware that even eighty-year-old grandmothers have been raped.

Many men respond as if they also feel the stress of our encounter. I've had large men hunch down, trying to look small and harmless, flashing me ear-to-ear grins and saying, "Hello. Have a nice day," in the reassuring tone one might use while trying not to alarm a feral cat. It helps, and I'm grateful for their sensitivity.

I dream of a time when all of us feel safe with each other and have abundant access to wilderness. There are organizations, such as Run Wild My Child, Outdoor Afro, and Latino Outdoors, helping families with young children and Black, Indigenous, and people of color to get out into nature. All of us deserve to spend time in nature as every culture around the world evolved with intimate contact with Earth. We all deserve the right to "sit back and watch the flowers grow . . . lay and watch the river flow," as India Arie sings in her song "Nature," from her debut studio album *Acoustic Soul*.

Henry David Thoreau's wise words resonate with me: "In wilderness is the preservation of the world." To preserve and restore ourselves, we need to preserve and restore the wild places, which can be medicine for everyone.

Forest Guidance

Vultures, like the condor I saw, who eat carrion, are chief among nature's recyclers and environmental clean-up crews. Nothing in nature is wasted. Nature recycles everything into new forms. Without recycling and composting, there would be no room on our planet for new life. A way that I have applied this in my personal life is a feng shui decluttering cure that creates more space in my life to birth my dreams. *Feng shui* is a Chinese term that means "wind-water" and gives techniques to create more energy flow in our homes and offices, similar to the way acupuncture creates more energy flow in our bodies. If you'd like to give this cure a try, then give away, compost, repair and reuse, recycle, or, as a last resort, throw away twenty-seven things for nine days. Ideas of what to get rid of include old medicines and vitamins, emails, files and paperwork, clothes you never wear, or anything you don't use and appreciate. You might even declutter your calendar to create more spaciousness in your life. Notice how you feel afterward. Do you have more energy to put into what you love?

10

Celtic Nature Magic

*There is magic in the rising moonlight, magic in the
way we take in cosmic energies through our bodies, cells
lighting up with conductive crystalline structures,
sacred geometries ignited in our blood.*

*Y*ears ago I was at Ancestor Tree, so named because of the
way the burled old tree spontaneously took me on a shamanic journey to meet my Celtic ancestress. I wasn't expecting to
go on a shamanic journey, although I have had a human practitioner
take me on them in the past. No one was drumming or rattling, and
I wasn't intending to visualize I was going down through Ancestor
Tree's roots into the underworld or up her trunk to the upper world,
as people often do with trees while journeying. But being with
ancient redwood trees is powerful and mysterious. Something about
their presence seems to not only connect the cosmic starry realms
with Earth but also to bridge time and space. Perhaps this is because
they are thousands of years old and have literally been here, on the
planet, for so long.

On that day, I had been circling around the tree saying prayers
when I suddenly saw a woman in a diaphanous white gown emerge
from the trunk and reach her hand out to me.

"I'm your Celtic ancestress," she says, "from your mother's line." Luminous sparkles swirl around her. "I've come across time," she adds, and somehow I realize she means hundreds of years, maybe even a thousand. She makes a beckoning gesture before fading back into the tree.

It's all so unexpected and a little bit overwhelming, this surprising vision. I lie down on the soft ground beside Ancestor Tree and breathe deeply into my chest and belly, trying to integrate what happened as I stare up at branches sweeping the sky. The air continues to shimmer with glittering light.

My hands seem to absorb the sparkles, and I feel my fingers vibrate. They look translucent. The word come, in the soft voice of my Celtic ancestress, whispers on the gentle wind. Suddenly, I sense my spirit body being carried down through the roots of Ancestor Tree into the underworld. A small black bear accompanies me on the journey, as I feel my hands hold onto the shallow roots before dropping down deeper into the underworld.

I am in another place and time. There is a ceremony around a huge old oak tree, which stands on a gently sloped, green grassy hill overlooking steep coves, a rocky shore, and a green-blue sea, frothy with white wave foam, which is a bit turbulent even on this calm day. It seems like the sort of place a mermaid might sun herself upon a rock. Women circle around the oak, dancing, laughing, singing, and making offerings of shells, feathers, and pebbles. In my spirit body, I walk up to them, and my Celtic ancestress holds her slender hands out to me, inviting me into the circle.

I notice her bare feet. It looks like little tendrils of light go from her soles right into the ground as she dances. As I circle and dance around the tree with the other women, I feel the love we share in our hearts, the mirth in our spirits, and our reverence for trees and stars. There is magic in the rising moonlight, magic in the way we take in cosmic energies through our bodies, cells lighting up with conductive crystalline structures, sacred geometries ignited in our blood. We weave the very fabric of our souls into this dance of life.

When I returned from that journey, I spent some time breathing and doing easy yoga beneath the trees, trying to figure out what had happened. It was wonderful and left me feeling great, but I didn't understand the experience.

As time has gone by, more of the puzzle pieces are coming together. Every once in a while when I am sitting with Ancestor Tree, I am swept back into a vision of being with my Celtic ancestress. So far, they have never been quite as powerful as that original meeting, where I actually felt my spirit body going into the tree. But sometimes I see pictures in my mind's eye of the simple wooden cottage where she lives. Drying herbs hang from the rafters. There's a porch and a nearby sparkling creek with leaping trout. I'd like to see more, but usually the images are a bit vague, like sketches or outlines. Along with the blurry images comes a knowing that this woman with the curly brown hair is offering to reconnect me with my genetic line of Celtic nature priestesses. That knowing is not blurry at all. I can't say exactly how I know; I just do. The same way I know the sky is blue or that I love my kids, I know my Celtic ancestress wants to share nature magic with me.

It's been lost and unraveled in my maternal line over many generations. There was too much trauma from invasion, colonization, and famine. We lost our knowledge and conscious connection to Earth intelligence. Fragments remained in the way my mother, aunt, and grandmother all loved to go outside for long walks and had a sixth sense and a quick intuition. My mother used to joke that she had eyes in the back of her head. And it was true. As a child, she always caught me immediately when I was trying to swipe an extra cookie or pretend I'd done my homework already so I could go out to play with my friends. I couldn't get away with anything! But there were no more ceremonies around a tree, no more consciously aligning with the elemental magic of Earth. Maybe, thanks to reconnecting with my Celtic ancestress, this deeper relationship with nature is coming more alive within me.

Forest Guidance

All of our ancestors evolved living closer to the natural world than most of us do now. They hunted, fished, gathered berries, grew crops, lived near fresh water, and made their clothes and homes from materials found close by on the land. Do you know who your ancestors were? What land did they live upon? What gifts from your ancestors' intimate connection with nature are coming down from your genetic lineage? Have you learned special recipes or ways to nurture and teach children? Did your great-grandmother know about herbs and now you find you also share this interest? Did she have a sixth sense like mine? Were there pithy sayings full of wisdom often repeated in your family? Close your eyes for a moment and imagine one of your ancestors beckoning to you. He or she wants to give you a gift that will enhance your relationship with nature. Allow this gift to slowly appear in your mind's eye. If nothing comes right away, have confidence that it will come soon in a dream or from something you read, hear, or see. For me it came in the image of a smooth mango seed, and I sensed it was the star seed of my soul. In that dreamy vision, I planted the seed beneath Ancestor Tree. When I visit the old tree, I now have a sense of homecoming and wonder if it is related to that planted mango seed. I still have no idea why it was such an unlikely seed, as mangos certainly do *not* grow in the redwoods.

11
Power Spots

Sitting down, I inhale the sweetness of
Ancestor Tree's immense presence.

After the vision of my Celtic ancestress, I visit Ancestor Tree often, hoping I will meet up with her again. As I tromp down the trail to the tree, I realize that it has been over a year since I've had even a glimmer of her. I wish she'd come and at least tell me her name. But so far she never has.

And, anyway, the biggest magic is getting to be here, in this untouched forest where trees murmur hushed secrets to the wind. A wildlife biologist friend told me they sighted a marten. It was the first one seen in over forty years. I can't help wishing I would see it too, but I'm not sure exactly where it is. Even if I knew the exact location, I probably still wouldn't find the martin. Martins are elusive and seldom seen. Pictures of the weasel-like animal are cute, with their luxurious bushy tails.

Rounding a bend, I catch a glimpse of a bushy tail out of the corner of my eye as something scampers across the trail. Staring, I hold my breath, hoping that my wish was granted and this is the martin. More magical things than that have happened to me in this forest. But it's a squirrel. I admire the animal's healthy coat of gray fur for a while. I don't see them as often as the ubiquitous golden-brown chipmunks.

Making my way to Ancestor Tree, I greet her with a bow. "How are you today?" I ask. "In the very same spot as usual," I make-believe she replies.

"Yes. I always know where to find you!" I continue my imaginary conversation while taking my boots off.

Sitting down, I inhale the sweetness of Ancestor Tree's immense presence. When I shut my eyes and meditate for a good long while, I begin to hear what sounds like indistinguishable voices talking above my head. I wonder if what I'm listening to are some sort of low-frequency energies from the environment, as I've read meditating can open us up to those. But I did not read that we can actually hear them. What I do remember reading in David E. Young's book *The Mouse Woman of Gabriola* is that mingled with the energy in our own brains, these low frequencies can convey healing throughout our bodies. Does it work when the sounds are practically inaudible? Perhaps this is another example of something similar to the way homeopathy works, where less is more and the smallest titration of a substance often has the biggest results. Could the smallest, almost imperceptible sounds have the most powerful effects upon our bodies or our consciousness?

I concentrate on the almost voices. At first I can't make out the words, which sound like they are coming through a radio station not quite tuned in. And then, loud and clear, I hear the phrase, "She's one of the old ones. Elen of the Ways."

My name is Ellen. Are these nonphysical beings speaking about me?

I try to picture who is speaking, what she looks like, but the inner screen of my mind remains black. I continue breathing and wait, curious if I will "hear" more.

I don't, but a mental image of a woman's hand holding out an egg begins to take shape. The egg is blue, striated with different shades ranging from turquoise to violet. The hand is slender and looks the same as the hand the woman in my original vision of my Celtic ancestress held out to me when she invited me into the circle of dancing women. "You're back!" I exclaim, feeling ecstatic to finally encounter her again. She places the metaphysical egg into my right palm. It feels so real that I can almost bend my fingers around the smooth marble-like surface. "Can you tell me your name?" I ask.

I hear faint laughter but no name. She whispers very faintly in my ear, "Come back with a friend. You can't do this by yourself."

"Do what?" There is no answer, although I sense elementals dancing about with the sheer joy of creative expression that is life. I wait for another hour, but my Celtic ancestress does not return.

Home again, I'm blown away to discover in Caroline Wise's book *Finding Elen: The Quest for Elen of the Ways* that there is an Elen of the Ways who was a goddess of the forest. I don't recall ever hearing about her before and am thrilled to learn she may have been one of the earliest goddesses in Britain. It is believed she dates back to the Paleolithic. Elen is an antlered deer goddess. This makes sense as deer were a primary means ancient people in that area supported themselves, using hides for clothing and shelter, bones for tools, and meat for food. Deer even guided them during seasonal migrations. Elen is also known as the Green Lady, and I marvel at the way I first heard of this ancestral forest goddess here, in another forest, far away across time and space.

Elen, the Deer Mother Goddess, becomes the Welsh Saint Elen, who was the patron saint for road builders and travelers and was known for her light. My name, Ellen, means "light." I've always been happy with my name and felt like it was right for me. At the suggestion of an editor who complained that too many people came up when someone googled Ellen Davidson, I began using my middle name, Dee. The name Dee means "dark waters." Light and dark waters is an even better fit for me; I've chosen to live my life as lightly and joyfully as possible even though I've spent much of my life diving into the dark waters of the unconscious, subconscious, and emotions.

Elen of the Ways certainly guides travelers along paths, physically and spiritually. As guardian of the leys, the old pathways and energies flowing around Earth, Elen knows the way. Sometimes these ways are waterways.

The leys are what many now call ley lines and are somewhat similar to the energetic meridians in the human body used by acupuncturists for healing purposes. There are as yet no scientific measurements to verify the existence of ley lines, although there is a proven geomagnetic field that originates in Earth's interior and extends into space. Until recently, there was also no scientific evidence to prove the efficacy of acupuncture, but it's hard to believe that over a billion Chinese using the procedure for thousands of years could all be wrong! New discoveries are backing up this anecdotal evidence. Science writer Catherine Caruso notes in an article for the Harvard Medical School that researchers have discovered that acupuncture does stimulate the body's anti-inflammatory response. Perhaps soon science will discover Earth's geomagnetic fields are somehow related to the lore of ley lines.

According to the lore of ley lines, places where they come together are often called power spots and are said to both heal people as well as guide them on shamanic journeys. Power spots are believed to be similar to the seven powerful energy centers, or chakras, in the human body. I can't help wondering if maybe Ancestor Tree is on a place where the ley lines converge in a power spot. I've certainly received healing energy, inspiration, guidance, stimulated imagination, visionary experiences, and even that one spontaneous shamanic journey at Ancestor Tree.

If this is a power spot, it is not well known like the major ones of Glastonbury and Stonehenge, England; Sedona, Arizona; Haleakala Volcano, Hawaii; the Great Pyramid of Giza, Egypt; Mayan ruins in Tulum, Mexico; and Mount Shasta, California. Mount Shasta is about a five-hour drive away from me and, according to Young, reputedly related to the fifth (throat) chakra, which stimulates creative expression. Others have called it the first (root) chakra or the sixth (third eye) chakra. The one thing all the spiritual traditions seem to agree on is that Mount Shasta is a power spot.

In the human body, we have the seven main energy centers, but there are also more minor ones. Possibly Ancestor Tree, where my clairvoyant and visionary sixth chakra is so activated, is on one of those. What if we all could find little power spots close to our homes that resonate with us personally and help us to receive powerful healing energies?

Forest Guidance

Follow your intuition to find your power spot. What kind of landscape surrounds you where you live? Even if you live in a big city, is it within the desert or by a beach, rainforest, mountain, prairie, bay, ocean, or river? We are usually in some resonance with the land where we live. We shower or bathe in the water, breathe the air, and walk on the ground, even if it is paved. So most of us may find we are drawn to elements found right in our nearby environments. Is there a rock or tree that you feel good being around? Do you yearn for a day at the beach? The places where we feel the best are the ones that are usually powerful for us because they help us relax and open up so that we can receive more energy and be nourished. Animals can be sensitive to energy, so notice where your pets feel good and want to go. Conversely, pay attention when your dog, horse, or cat does not want to go someplace! Electromagnetic currents run everywhere through Earth's body, and we pick these up whether or not we are conscious of it. Most people know they feel much better after a day at the beach. Without any effort at all, natural places like this clear our auras and energetic fields, and we literally brighten up.

12
Sixth Sense

It is always easier to feel subtle energies
with the help of the ancient trees.

At the trees, I was "told" to come back with a friend. Now I
have to find someone. It's not always easy. Not everyone
wants to hike eight miles with me and also spend a couple of hours
meditating with a tree. Fortunately, Allegra awakens the next morning
with the guidance that she needs to go to the trees.

So we set off for Ancestor Tree. Although it is always easier to
feel subtle energies with the help of the ancient trees, neither of us is
prepared for what happens when we arrive at the tree and close our
eyes to meditate.

"I saw us back in Ireland with that group of women again, dancing
around the oak tree," I say.

"So did I!" exclaims Allegra. "It was some sort of ceremony. They
were chanting poetry."

"Yes!" I'm excited. I heard the poetry too, although I couldn't
understand the Gaelic words. We compare our visions, and Allegra
describes the tree on the cliffs by the sea. Perhaps it is not surprising our visions are identical. Allegra's ancestry is similar to mine. She
also descends from Celts and Russians, although I add Germans and
Bulgarians into the mix.

Both of us describe an intelligent, alive light traveling across time and continents, connecting us with our Celtic ancestral lines. Pulsating waves of high-frequency energy look like the beam of a flashlight. I inhale the light, imbibe it through my pores, quenching a thirst I did not know I had. Along with the light comes awareness that nature magic was at the very heart and core of Celtic spirituality—working with the elements and seasons, communicating with plants and animals, listening to birds, and honoring life. Once again, I catch a mental glimpse of my ancestress offering me the blue egg and hear her whisper in my mind, "Elen." What is this egg? Eggs are a symbol of fertility, new beginnings, and unhatched potential. Why does my ancestress want me to have it? Is my ancestress giving me a new potential? Something from the distant past she wants carried on into the future?

Years pass and I notice magic entering my life in lots of little ways. At first it's almost imperceptible, but the synchronicities and coincidences pile up. I try to remember, but I don't think I always lived this way, where I happen to be in the right place and time so often. Over and over again, the camping trips I planned weeks or months in advance land on the week with perfect weather, and then I hear friends complain about being caught in torrential downpours the day after I left. It happens so much that Allegra and I name it, "The luck of the elves." It occurs to me that when we vow our service to Earth or any aspect of her, we are often blessed with help in all sorts of ways from the elementals.

Many of my prayers are answered. Throughout my years of jaunting about the woods, I've often run into animals. Otters, squirrels, and deer delight me, but sometimes the animals are scary. I've rounded bends in trails and nearly bumped into black bears or suddenly come across a mountain lion. These meetings are awesome moments of complete presence but also quite terrifying. After seeing several mountain lions, I was beginning to think I might have to give up hiking alone. But I love the silence and peace of being by myself in the woods. I slow down and become more aware of everything around me. No way do I want to have to find someone to go with me each time. Besides, who is going to go three days a week?

So one day I sit down by a gigantic tree and tune in. Once I am in resonance, I say a prayer that I will no longer see any animals that scare me while I am out here alone. Many years later, I still haven't seen another lion or bear while I'm alone. Lion scat and tracks are often on the riverbanks, and the piles of bear poop are unmistakable; the animals are still out here. Once, when Allegra was meditating on the other side of a giant tree from me, a bear clomped all around making quite a racket but remaining concealed by the brush. He showed himself only on her side of the tree. Although I heard the bear thrashing about, I never saw him! Once again my messages at the trees were confirmed.

An odd coincidence that I am still doubting could possibly be real is that the local weather seems to be cooperating with me. When I'm outside and it looks like rain, if I don't have my raincoat and rain pants and am worried I'll be soaked and chilled, I ask if the rain can hold off an hour or two until I reach the car. It has been doing so every single time. Even though I still don't quite believe I can possibly have any influence on the weather and wouldn't count on or expect this to work, the every single time is catching my attention. I wonder if it continues on for years or decades, at what point I may decide even the weather is an interactive relationship?

Listening to my intuition has become second nature. Allegra and I call this, "Move the car," because once when she was parked beside the community forest, she heard the words in her head, "Move the car." Looking around, Allegra didn't see any reason she had to move her car. She was parked legally, and there were no threats. Feeling tired, Allegra ignored the voice and shut her eyes for a few moments, waiting for her daughter to get out of art camp. She was abruptly startled when another car bashed into hers.

Now when we hear these voices, we pay attention. The thing is, when we do move our cars and prevent whatever was about to happen, we never know what it is that we missed. But after paying the price of not listening enough times, we've learned that when the voice in our heads tells us to move the car, we'd better move it. How many of us have been taught to rationalize and invalidate these quick intuitive impulses? How different would our lives be if we learned to be guided by this "something more"?

A moment of synchronicity happened yesterday. I was writing the section about Elen of the Ways, when my friend thought of me and sent a video about Elen of the Ways. She had no idea I was writing about Elen. The information was exactly what I needed to share in this book. The facts about ants seeding trilliums appeared in a similar way right as I was describing the trillium-clad trail. Writing this book is larger than my personal self. I'm not so much writing it as receiving it.

My sixth sense sometimes includes an intuitive knowing about which plants, herbs, and mushrooms to eat. Maybe our ancestors also used this intuitive sense to figure out plants that were safe to ingest. It's hard to believe it was all trial and error, with people dying constantly from eating the wrong mushrooms and berries. It's a two-way street because many times I can also hear the plants telling me what they need as well. It's usually water, sunshine, or nutrients for the soil, but sometimes they want a little love, appreciation, and attention.

Plants aren't the lone ones speaking in my head. Since receiving the gift of Celtic nature magic, I often hear a sentence in my mind a few seconds before a person says that exact sentence. It's a bit uncanny. I'd love to know how many others are experiencing this and what they make of it.

Recently, I heard an interview with a psychiatrist on the radio. I didn't catch his name, but he was saying that about one in ten people hear voices. If they aren't saying horrible things and disrupting a person's life, he claimed it wasn't a mental health problem. I have permission from the doctor to listen to the tree dryads and flower fairies, I think, laughing. On a more serious note, it is refreshing and relieving to hear that unexplained perception is no longer all categorized as a psychiatric disorder. Many writers I know hear the voices of their characters talking in their heads, accents and all.

Forest Guidance

Do you have a sixth sense? How does it show up in your life? Have there been times where you haven't listened to your intuition and later regretted it? If you would like to open up a more intuitive ability to commune with nature, the first thing to do is to "Be With." Drop all preconceptions and expectations and allow yourself to notice how you feel in the presence of a rock, tree, river, or whatever aspect of the wild world where you are most attracted. Often information comes into us more as sensation than in words. Later it might become conscious as some of the huge amount of information our bodies are picking up makes its way into our intellects. Nature therapy opens us up to our higher guidance. According to Dr. Sue Morter in her book *The Energy Codes*, the soul informs the body, and then, if our minds don't invalidate or override the information, our bodies share the information with our brains. There are stories of people receiving information directly from nature. Ancient Celts indicated that their whole ogham alphabet, mostly named after trees, was discerned by a man who heard them by listening to the songs of the universe. Diana Beresford-Kroeger writes in her book *To Speak for the Trees* that ogham characters were carved into large rectangular limestones, and people were said to be able to communicate with these stones.

13
Pink Silk Dress

*If I were to see myself as beautiful and exquisite and
having something unique to offer, wouldn't I deserve to
treasure myself for exactly who I am? Don't we all?*

A highly intuitive man who has studied the Kabbalah gave
me a psychic healing. He told me that I was like a pink silk
dress that had been put in the dryer with the dungarees and that I'd
had the wrong upbringing for my temperament. His words made me
flash back to how, back in the 1950s and 1960s, my parents along with
many others believed that children were like raw clay that could be
molded into any shape.

It took a lot of energy exploring all these ideas other people had
of who and what I was supposed to be. For years, it felt like trying on
dozens of different outfits. No, I'm not this one. Not that one. Some
of them I even wore for a while, like being a nurse, before realizing
what a bad fit it was. Trying to be a nurse was ridiculous for me. I run
at the first sight of blood—even sometimes when my kids were young
and needed a Band-Aid. Well, some years into the parenting gig, I did
learn to put on the Band-Aids, but it did not come easily. I tried to be
so many things parents, teachers, and cultural conditioning told me
that I was or should be, that I had very little vitality left to look within
and feel into who I actually was.

So the image of the pink silk dress stuck with me. Most of my life, I'd been trying to fit in, trying to be tough enough not to let the loud, frenetic pace of our modern life bother me. Like many, I over-rode my inner reality so that I could conform. When it didn't work, I blamed myself. My inner critic beat me up, calling me "too sensitive" and "selfish" when I said no to events that felt stressful. I felt guilty for not showing up for people as much as I thought I should. Of course, I realize now that no matter how hard I try, I'm never going to be any good at being someone else—but like all of us I can become great at being me.

The psychic's picture of me as a pink silk dress gave me a new way to see myself. What if, instead of not being good enough, I was actually like that dress? Of course I'd take care of my luscious dress by hanging it carefully inside a garment bag, wearing it only to fancy events and not to clean the house or hike in the woods. If I were to see myself as beautiful and exquisite and having something unique to offer, wouldn't I deserve to treasure myself for exactly who I am? Don't we all? And we are not all the same, so our needs are going to be vastly different. No one besides ourselves is living in our bodies, and no one else can tell us what it is we need to flourish.

According to Elaine N. Aron in her book *The Highly Sensitive Person*, about 20 percent of the population is considered highly sensitive. We pick up more and therefore need more down time to sort through all the information we've absorbed. Although sometimes it makes it a little more challenging to cope with the hurly-burly speed, clamor, and flashing lights of modern life, being sensitive in wilderness is a profound gift. There is so much subtle intelligence to perceive. All humans have the capacity to cultivate sensitivity. Trees can help us do this.

Perhaps because most of humanity evolved with forests, our nervous systems are wired to feel comfortable in the forest. But for many of us the forest or any place in wild nature is now an unfamiliar environment, and we tend to feel afraid of the unknown. So although our nervous systems are genetically wired to be in natural surroundings, we may have to retrieve our sense of relaxation and belonging. This can be done by going often so that our chosen environment becomes known and familiar. It may also help to have trusted companions or guides. When we feel safe in our surroundings, then we can relax and enjoy the shapes and shadows instead of feeling afraid. We can feel peaceful as we listen to mist dripping on fronds and notice shafts of light streaming through trees. We can discover that part of ourselves that is open to being at home in nature.

This sort of openness is an automatic doorway into sensitivity. Perhaps it is a quality in our genetics that can be turned off or on, depending upon our circumstances. When we are in environments that call us, entice us with beauty, invite our presence, so that we are seduced into unfurling our tightly clenched selves, we mingle more consciously with our shared biological world. There's intelligence all about. We learn from earthworms and fungi, faint sounds, the whispers of our hearts, and the *wise field*, a term I first learned from Justine Toms of New Dimensions Radio. When I asked her what she meant by the term, she said, "The wise field is a field in which we are all born into and exist within. We live in a net of intelligent communion where all life is connected and reciprocal. It is the inescapable mutuality of the larger, more inclusive field that our human bodies are made of and which is of the same substance with all life. In this field we resonate and vibrate as we share the same source and the same elements as the stars."*

Before my interview with Justine, I think we connected through this inclusive field. She had not told me in advance what questions she planned to ask. Since I had no idea what to expect, I went to the trees and allowed my thoughts to ramble. When the interview happened,

---

*From email correspondence, August 7, 2023.

I was surprised to discover that those rambling thoughts were the answers to almost every single one of her questions! Later when I complimented Justine on her great questions, she replied that she received what to ask from the wise field. The old trees connected me with Justine in that field. This sort of unity consciousness is available for all of us when we spend time developing our sensitivity and tuning in. It's a lot easier to do so with the nature support of wild places.

Forest Guidance

Sitting with trees, especially old ones, is a powerful practice to both open our sensitivity and soothe our systems. First ask the tree if you have permission to connect. If you receive the open, expansive feeling of a yes, then find a comfortable spot near the tree. Trees have a radiant field, and it is not necessary to actually touch the tree. Begin by breathing deeply. Take your shoes off and touch the soles of your feet and then the ground. This will help you connect with the earth and root into the soil beside the tree. Notice how you slow down and come into rhythm with the tree. Do you feel calmer? From this relaxed state, invite in communication or guidance from the larger wise field. Relax and allow yourself to perceive without preconceptions or expectations. You may not at first realize that you've received anything important. I certainly did not before my interview with Justine; I thought my mind was randomly drifting around with all sorts of thoughts. Trust that whatever you do receive is what you need right now, even if it is tingling in your toes. There are subtle ways that we come more alive when we are in direct contact with nature.

14
Lion

*Loping lithely, the lion moves with such elegance
that she looks as sinuous as a river,
a winding flow of pure motion.*

*O*ut in the wild woods being open and sensitive is certainly a blessing. Sometimes I've even dreamed of landscapes, including details of waterfalls, flowers, the color of the rocks, or a specific tree, and then later found myself in exactly that spot. It feels like déjà vu and makes me ponder if it is actually the place that called me there, or if it was somehow known like fate that I would be in that spot.

During the Awakening Women Sadhana I previously mentioned, where we delved into the goddess Freyja, I learned that in Norse mythological tradition, fate is called *orlaeg* (also spelled *orlog* or *orlay*). It's also defined as "first law" or "primary layer." The orlaeg is the original instructions for an individual and includes their gender, race, and ethnicity and the place, time, culture, and other specific conditions of their birth. Though 20 percent of the orlaeg cannot be changed, the other 80 percent is the result of choices an individual makes. It helps when we make our choices based on our heart and soul passions. These are easier to find in the silence and peace of a forest.

Steve and I stop at a cascade of sparkling water. Before filling our canteens, I say thank you to the guardian of this rivulet. I don't actually perceive anyone, but it is always respectful to ask permission and say thanks before taking anything, and the water looks delicious. We treat it with our UV light filters to prevent infections from bacteria like giardia. Before taking a sip, I wonder what this little creek will taste like. Each water source has a distinctive flavor, and water tasting has become something of a hobby for me and Steve, sort of like wine tasting. We drink, swishing the water around in our mouths. Swallowing, I observe, "Tastes earthy."

"Minerals," agrees Steve, and we try to figure out if it's sodium, iron, or calcium.

"Seems a little minty too," I add.

Steve points to some pennyroyal growing beside the whitewater rills spraying over a rock.

I nod, thinking about how different this water is from the water that comes out of our taps. Masaru Emoto in his book *The Hidden Messages in Water* showed that water funneled through pipes and treated with chemicals is unable to form complete crystals. The crystals are flattened and distorted, their crystalline structure altered. Naturally flowing water is filtered through the earth, plants, and stones. The crystals in this pure water usually maintain a hexagonal shape, which is a sacred geometry found throughout nature, showing up in snowflakes, corals, and the honeycombs of bees.

Perhaps drinking this water is similar to taking a homeopathic remedy where the barest essence of a substance can have the most powerful healing influence on the body. Are the crystalline structures in this one small sip of water informing my own fluid body, the 70-plus percent of myself made of water? Are my internal waters coming into some sort of deeper resonance with the primeval beauty all around me and forming hexagonal crystals? I feel like I'm drinking a magical elixir!

Steve and I start walking again, and my thoughts ramble faster than my feet. Being in wilderness helps us come into our core essences as well as to expand further out into the connected whole. For sensitive people, power comes from listening to ourselves, going within and paying attention. Power comes from trusting and believing in ourselves; we are all our own authorities on how we feel and perceive. Power comes when we value our own inner guidance foremost, so that we walk with the assured grace and poise of lions.

Stepping confidently on the narrow trail that winds around a steep ravine, I playact walking with the poise and grace of a lion, imagining I have a tail acting like a rudder, balancing me and keeping me in touch with the ground. Perhaps thinking of lions is precognitive, because the next thing I know, a mountain lion comes bounding around the curving path on the other side of the gulch. I gasp. "A lion!" Steve and I freeze. Gaps in the trees give us a clear view.

The tawny lion streaks along the footpath opposite us. Loping lithely, the lion moves with such elegance that she looks as sinuous as a river, a winding flow of pure motion. We are awed and still far enough away not to feel too scared. Leaping up a small hill that overlooks the trail, the lion moves out of view.

"Wow!" We both say at once. "That was amazing!"

And then Steve points. "We have to walk right past that outcropping."

He is right. Our way to the car switchbacks right underneath the hill where the lion disappeared. For all we know, the lion is hunched up there, ready to pounce on our backs. Lions usually do attack from the rear. "There's no other way back." My heart beats fast and my mouth is so dry I can barely swallow. Steve and I both know about the lion that jumped on a man in this forest years ago. His wife bravely fought the lion off by poking her pen into the lion's eyes.

Licking my dry lips, I say, "I'm scared."

"Let's wait here for a moment and give the lion time to move off," suggests Steve. Squinting, I stare up at the lion's slope, looking for any hint of that tawny-gold body. I don't see anything, but my heart is still thumping away.

After five minutes that feel like forever, Steve says, "The lion is probably gone. It's probably not stalking us. There are so many deer around that I doubt they are going after people."

"Yeah," I say, looking nervously at the dusky sky. "We're going to have to go soon or it will be dark before we reach the car."

We stand as tall as we can and sing loudly, clacking our poles and making a racket as we creep around the bend that could have a lion right above. I'm listening so hard that I hardly breathe when we make it past the place where the lion vanished.

As soon as we are out of sight of the promontory, clad in huckleberry shrubs and redwood trees, I sigh with relief. "Whew!" My hands are shaking. At least I wasn't hiking alone. My prayer to not see scary animals out here when I'm alone must still be working.

"That was intense!" says Steve.

We are safe. We are alive. Should I say a new prayer, not to see any scary animals at all, even when I am with a companion? Chewing on my bottom lip, I'm not sure. The lion was magnificent. I'll never forget the smooth way the animal moved.

That night, I dream of a huge, golden African lioness who cuddles me close to her heart. I'm enfolded in luscious fur. Warm. Soft. I'm a little scared, but I know this lioness is an ally.

A few nights later, I have a second lion dream. This time, a white African lioness charges me and Steve. I get behind a glass door, but Steve hesitates and the lioness bounds in before he can shut it. I step back behind a second, inner glass door and do close it, knowing glass is not much protection from a powerful lioness. I feel scared, and the dream borders on nightmare.

The dream was so vivid that when I awaken, I know I need to dive deeper into it to discern what my consciousness is trying to tell me. Using one of my favorite techniques to decode dreams, I become the lioness from my oneiric state, getting down on all fours, moving like a lioness, roaring a bit, and speaking from her voice. When I do, I realize the lioness was not trying to hurt me. She was running toward me as if I were her precious cub. She is a second ally.

After both of these dreams, I am left with the impression that there's a white lioness walking beside me on my left side and a golden lioness on the right. Walking with metaphysical lions, my feet feel confident and secure on the ground.

Forest Guidance

Every creature has an important place in the web of life. Lions are predators. Predators are essential to maintain the balance because otherwise we'd be overrun with everything from deer to mosquitoes. Similarly, we all have our valuable place in life. Take a moment to feel into your solar plexus, the area above the belly button and below the rib cage, where the chakra that most represents power is located. Allow this area to expand and open. Maybe imagine you have a power animal looking out from your solar plexus chakra. Who would it be? Whale, owl, eagle, ant, snail, or fish, they all have powerful teachings to convey. Whatever creature comes to you, think about the associations you have with it, the qualities it holds for you, and how your power animal reveals an aspect of your own power. Many people have shared with me that they have found their one power animal, a singular guide, such as a raven or a panther, but that has not been my experience. Various power animals have shown up as guides for me at different times in my life. As well as the recent lions, I've worked with a snowy white owl, an eagle, a green sea turtle, a whale, a bear, otters and dolphins, and quite often a little green frog. The frog helps me clear my aura and sometimes grows big and fat feasting on my negative thoughts!

15
Gravity

*Bears must be feeling Earth's changes, living in caves or
under logs, nestled into the ground, sleeping
deep in the heartbeat of Mother.*

*F*eet on the ground. Held close to Mother Earth. Held by her gravity.

Alone today in the redwoods. A misty, drippy gray day with the soft touch of fog on my cheeks. Lately, I haven't been able to spend as many days alone out here as usual. The winter weather was often too harsh, even for me, with high winds howling through the forest. And when it was finally calm enough to hike, Steve and Allegra usually wanted to go with me. I love their company and we are all silent for a good part of the hike, but my introverted self needs some time being alone out in the woods.

Completely undistracted, I connect to the trees in a deeper way. There's no hold on my receiving, no fear of being too altered, and my consciousness expands. First, I often set up a safe container for myself. It's a hodgepodge I've learned over the years from my eclectic California background and has grown rather elaborate. I know it's a quirky way to set up my spiritual journeys, and I break rules by not following one specific tradition. But I have been consistently going deep into my wild path, and part of the charm of that is to do things in my own wild way.

For me this works so well that I hesitate to change a thing. I'll share my process here.

Sitting quietly in the forest, I gaze upon my surroundings, which could be mossy green rocks, woods' rose shrubs with dainty pink blossoms, or logs covered in lichen. The soothing forest embraces me. Feeling the security of being enfolded in this quiet, protected world, I begin. I've found it is more powerful to say, sing, or chant the words aloud.

Clear light surrounds me. Nothing but good comes to me. Nothing but good goes from me. I give thanks. I fully embody my higher self, Ellen Dee Davidson. A crystal light Star of David surrounds me and a *merkaba*—a light vehicle made out of love that protects my frequency. I connect to my earth star chakra, which helps me to be in touch with the electromagnetic waves of Gaia. Below that, I visualize a crystalline platform. A grounding cord goes from the platform into the heart of Mother Earth. I share my essence with Earth and imbibe her frequencies, calibrated and filtered through the platform and my earth star chakra. They are the ones I need now. Taking this energy up through my chakras, I open my seventh crown chakra. Above, I connect with my soul star chakra and another clear crystalline platform. A beam of light connects me from there to my star family.

Now I feel like I am similar to the giant redwood trees, lined up between the starry heavens and Earth. Next I put a circle around the column of light. This includes archangels, my own personal team named Fairy Bells, of course (are you laughing?), Gaia and the elementals, tree spirits, benevolent ancestors, whichever power animals wish to assist me, and various other goddesses and guides.

I ask for a full mind, body, spirit, and emotional clearing on
all levels and dimensions, all realities and parallel realities,
whether I know about them or not. I ask that all my chakras
be uncorded and cleared. I fill with the most beautiful colors, frequencies, sounds, and vibrations for every chakra and
layer of my aura, in harmony within themselves and with one
another.

After this, blessing energies come into my wide open field. Sometimes
I do it with Steve or Allegra, giving them both room to custom-tailor
their light cocoons—adding personal spiritual elements and taking out
parts that don't resonate with them. They both tell me that they definitely feel the difference afterward, which is a surprising admission on
my husband's part since he is not into all my "woo-woo" stuff.

Once I feel myself in the high-vibration egg of beautiful radiant
light, I often perceive an odd hum in the forest. It's not always the
same. Sometimes it is a low-toned murmur, sometimes the sound is so
high pitched it sounds like the silvery chime of a bell.

Gliding through the green understory, enjoying the pungent smell
of California bay laurels, I notice there's no one else around. I certainly don't want to run into another lion when I'm out here alone! I
need my bear bell. The bell warns lions as well as bears that someone
is coming, and they usually stay well out of sight. But I lost my bear
bell again. The ringing annoys Steve, so I take it off my poles when he
hikes with me. Then I lose it.

Bears are waking up from hibernation now and are active. Allegra
showed me a picture of a cinnamon-colored black bear she recently
encountered, and the expression in the bear's eyes was disgruntled. We
figured it was probably a rough winter for bears and other animals,
with trees crashing down all around in the forest. Most likely the poor

bear didn't get the refreshing sleep of a normal hibernation. Bears must be feeling Earth's changes, living in caves or under logs, nestled into the ground, sleeping deep in the heartbeat of Mother. Intuitively, I feel the bears wanting me to share their distress over the droughts, fires, floods, and tumbling trees this stormy winter. "I'm so sorry," I whisper, promising that I will write this in my book.

Singing to let the bears and lions know I'm around, I make my way past sparkling creeks and up slopes thick with trees. After a few miles, I come to a side trail with an as-yet unnamed tree where I often sit. Here I root in, allowing Earth to hold me. She holds me with her gravity. Gravity is one of those laws of nature that are irrefutable. Gravity is not a fixed and steady state but instead a dynamic process. A 2023 article in the *Washington Post*, by Joel Achenback and Victoria Jaggard, reported recent evidence of a "gravitational wave background." Massive celestial objects, including black holes, interact and send low-frequency gravitational waves rippling through space-time, which cause Earth to bobble on the fluctuating seas of the universe.

Bobbling or not, gravity is probably the most coherent force we know, holding masses together. Even our language shows respect for the seriousness of gravity: gravitas, grave, gravitate. Is gravity the 20 percent of Earth's orlaeg—her fate or destiny—that is a fixed law and cannot be changed? Does Earth, like us, have free will? Possibly this is another fractal pattern, repeating on many levels. If we have orlaeg, as Nordic mythology suggests, it doesn't seem too far-fetched to me to think that Earth may have similar laws.

Certainly, the law of gravity is the force that keeps all the planets orbiting around the sun. It is the force that holds me close to Earth. What a nice thing to know that no matter what I do, I'm not going to fall off! Mama has me. Anything that has mass—the amount of matter in an object—also has gravity. Earth has more mass than I do, and so her pull upon me is greater than mine upon her. It's interesting to think that we are also pulling on Earth. Does she feel us?

And does this tree at my back feel my gravitational pull? I certainly feel the pull of the tree, sinking into an embrace that holds me. Part of being able to open up to nonordinary reality comes from this feeling of being held. When we feel safe, we can allow ourselves to let go and unclench. We can melt into the moment. We can receive.

Today what I receive is peace. Simple peace. Breathing. Presence. Calm. Relaxation. It's fun to write about exciting meditations, where I have visions and the fireworks are sparking. But this wordless calm is priceless. My skull relaxes. My head feels spacious and opens like a flower in the sun. Recharging energy pours in, and I stretch and sigh with pleasure, my soft animal body glowing with renewal. Whatever is grave and serious in our lives, heavy and incontrovertible, can be made more comfortable when we allow ourselves to both settle into the reality of gravity—we are here now, being held on our one precious planet—while receiving the cosmic rays from our universe made of love.

Forest Guidance

Find a comfortable place to rest upon the ground. Perhaps put a blanket or beach towel down, preferably made of natural fiber like cotton, which is more conductive of Earth's electromagnetic energies than materials like plastic. Allow yourself to sink in, relaxing all your muscles, breathing into your toes, ankles, knees, thighs, hips, belly, back, chest, shoulders, neck, jaw, and temples and the top of your head. Melt even more deeply into the ground, observing the way gravity holds you. You don't have to try to hold yourself up. You are held in Mother Earth's embrace. Feel the way Earth loves you, a mama holding you close, like a bear in a cave. This sense of being held and able to let go was a big part of how forest bathing healed me, allowing tense muscles to relax. I would imagine Gaia's heartbeat lulling me as she may lull you too. Can you allow your own heartbeat to feel in rhythm with hers, the way the heartbeats of a baby synchronize with those of the mother? Can you imagine Gaia's heartbeat soothing you? "You belong to me," says Earth. "You are welcome here."

16
Graves

Ancient trees have the ability to help us
expand perception beyond the physical
into multidimensional realities.

It's not a big leap from gravity to graves. I wonder, have you ever been visited by someone after they died? I suspect this is more common than many of us realize. People confide privately about their experiences. One friend who was bereft when her mother died when she was twelve years old once told me that afterward her mother came to her in a dream and held her hand. Together, they flew up to a beautiful place. My friend said she felt blissful and full of love. Her mother told her, "This is as far as you can go. I wanted you to know that I'm OK." My friend wanted to stay there with her mom but was told, "You have to go back." When my friend woke up, she felt soothed and comforted.

Something similar happened to Allegra. A boyfriend from when she was young recently died. Although they'd both grown up and married other people, they did love each other. When he died, she had a vivid dream of meeting him on some boat docks. All the boats were lit up with lights, and he looked happy. He ran up some stairs, gesturing for her to come with him, but Allegra knew that she couldn't go further without giving up her life, which she wasn't ready to do.

A few years later, she had a second vision before a dear friend died. The last day Allegra saw her friend, a voice told her that this was the final time she'd ever see that friend. It didn't make sense to Allegra, since her friend was young and healthy, but she went back anyway and gave her friend a hug. The following morning, Allegra and her partner woke up in a room full of golden light. Their hearts were overflowing with love. Turning to her partner, Allegra said, "Somebody loves us!" Later that same day, they discovered their dear friend had fallen off a cliff and died. The golden light of love was Allegra's friend coming to say good-bye.

Another friend lost her husband, and every morning for months she'd wake up with the feeling he was right there beside her. One person told me that all the electronics in her house would flash, and then her skin would get goose bumps and she'd know her deceased husband was in the room with her. Someone else said he smelled his wife's perfume, when there was absolutely no perfume in the room.

I bet many of you either have a few stories of sensing people from the other side or else know someone who has. We tend not to talk about these stories much because they feel sacred. We don't want the tenderness and mystery we feel to be diminished by disbelief.

I've had these experiences quite a number of times when people in my circle have died. My aunt came to me in a dream after her death. She was building a boat to get to the other side. The boat was made out of all the good deeds she'd done in her life, all the people she'd helped in any way. She asked me for memories of when she'd been kind or helpful to me.

Soon after my husband's mother passed on, she came to me in a vision, shaking her head, dumbfounded, and told me she'd never understood my sensitivity and hadn't realized that I was "walking two worlds." Somehow in the vision she conveyed a sense of being impressed that I could live here while somehow staying open to the dimensions of spirit. Occurrences like the ones above as well as many people's reported near-death experiences indicate that we don't completely cease to exist after we die.

Five years ago my father died. We shared our love for the mountains, and I always felt very close to him. He came to me when I was meditating at Ancestor Tree. Although he didn't speak words, I felt his essence clearly along with a sense that he was offering to continue to help me on my life journey. In some inexplicable way, the old-growth redwood helped me to perceive my father.

Ancient trees have the ability to help us expand perception beyond the physical into multidimensional realities. This leads me to the exciting possibility of creating green burial groves, where the dead are buried beneath trees. In a green burial, there is no crypt, vault, toxic embalming fluid, or headstone. The body is buried in a simple shroud or biodegradable casket three to four feet below the surface, where it is allowed to decompose in the shelter of trees, becoming part of the root system and offering nutrients to the soil. When someone is buried in a root zone, rather than the conventional six feet down, their body literally becomes part of the living breathing tree, and so this is often called "entreement." Soil scientist Michael Furniss, shared with me that green burial is not actually new. It's how many of our ancestors buried people and is much healthier for the landscape, gifting the body to the earth organically. It's a lovely idea and completely in accord with the way the natural world constantly recycles, one thing morphing into another as we eat and are eaten, grow and die. Pets and placentas can also be buried in a green burial grove, and trees planted in honor of newborn babies, as well as the deceased, are also accepted. These groves become pleasant places for family and friends to visit their deceased loved ones and one another and enjoy themselves in a beautiful environment, where they can relax and even have picnics. Natural burial can also be done in grasslands and orchards.

The idea of being buried under a redwood or oak is enchanting. Symbolically to me, it feels like part of the movement to reconnect to Earth. How lovely to gift our bodies to soil and trees and create beautiful park-like settings where we can visit and commune with our entreed loved ones. Thanks to the hard work of many people, this is becoming an option. The goal of green burial sites is to bring the forest back to a diverse and healthy ecosystem, similar to that of old-growth forests.

Forest Guidance

When I am in nature, I often feel that my prayers are heard better—like an extra good phone connection. If you want to try to engage nature support in your prayers, go to a forest or your favorite nature spot. If you can't physically go there, imagine you are there in full, vivid detail. Notice all the sensory smells, sights, touches, tastes, and sounds. When you feel fully present in the scene, say a prayer for your departed loved one. It could be a person or a beloved pet, houseplant, or tree. Then allow yourself to drift into a state of open attention. Be aware of any changes you feel. These might include a sense of comfort, an idea about what you need to do next, a synchronicity, or even a visualization of your departed loved one. Have faith that whether you sense anything or not, your prayer went out to the universe in a wave of blessing.

17
Soil

*Over the course of fifty thousand years, about an inch of
burned-up meteor debris falls to the ground and
becomes part of the soil. We walk on stardust!*

*E*verything is so damp after the rains this year. It's already May,
and most days are still drizzly. Plants love it and look vibrant
and plumped up for the first time in years. I'm still rigged out in my
poncho and rain pants. In a way I love the inclement weather because
I have the trails to myself, and it is quiet other than the burble of the
creek, rustle of fronds, splish-splash of gently falling raindrops, and
the muted calls of returning songbirds. Careful not to tread on yellow
banana slugs, I hike deeper into the welcoming forest.

Rounding a bend, I see something small, fluffy, and white. It looks
like a stuffed animal, an owl. Perhaps a child dropped it, I think, hoping there's a lost and found at the visitors' center. I know from the way
my three-year-old granddaughter carries her favorite doll, Ari, everywhere, how a particular stuffed animal can be absolutely irreplaceable
to a child. There are no substitutes for Ari; no other doll or stuffed
animal will do. When Ari is missing, we search the house top to bottom. So I prepare to pick up the stuffed baby owl.

She moves.

I blink and stare. Did the owl really move?

The owl blinks back at me.

She's alive! What is she doing standing in the middle of the trail?

The owl tilts her head to one side watching me.

Tiptoeing around her, I watch her watch me, swiveling her head to keep me in view, puffing out her feathers and clack-clack-clacking her beak.

Could she be an endangered spotted owl? Probably not. There are only a few of those left in this forest. More likely she's one of the barred owls that have moved here from their disrupted habitats on the East Coast, where most old-growth forests have been logged. As Craig Welch notes in an article for the *Smithsonian Magazine*, the migrant barred owls are taking over the territory of the indigenous spotted owls.

Sitting down a few feet away from her, I think about what I should do. Is she hurt? Does she need help? She looks so soft. I yearn to reach my fingers out and gently stroke her downy feathers, but I don't want to touch her in case my scent on her feathers keeps her parents from picking her up. Maybe I should hike back to the visitors' center and tell one of the park rangers? I'm four miles into the forest and hope the owl will still be here by the time they get back to her. I hope she doesn't get eaten. She's adorable.

Keeping my gaze wide and unfocused, I look into her eyes in a desire to commune more deeply and perhaps understand what it is she needs. Her gaze is unfathomable, and her consciousness feels foreign to me. Still there is a sense of nonverbal communication. She stops clack-clacking and ruffling her feathers. Perhaps the clacking was a warning to scare me off or a call to her parents. A feeling of peace comes over me. What a blessing to be able to sit with a baby owl. After a timeless time looking at each other that feels like forever, I stand back up and whisper, "Stay safe, baby owl." No one is around, so I decide heading back to the visitors' center is my best option.

Talking to the ranger, I learn that sometimes baby barred owls do fall to the ground before they are ready to fly. Their parents watch out for them, and the baby owls are usually fine, as long as well-meaning humans don't pick them up or try to rescue them. Whew! I'm relieved to know that I made the right decision. It was a close call. Sometimes we want to help, but our ignorance can make us do the exact wrong thing. Glad I dodged that mistake, I slip back into the forest. It's still early afternoon, and I'm not ready to go home yet.

The damp soil smells so good. Soil is such a foundation for life. I read recently that it takes ten or even twenty thousand years to form one foot of soil. Topsoil is ancient and alive. As Michael Furniss notes in his article "Fundament Wonder," soil is made of minerals, bacteria, fungi, insects, insect droppings, and stardust.

Hard to wrap our minds around the fact that soil is literally stardust. Over the course of fifty thousand years, about an inch of burned-up meteor debris falls to the ground and becomes part of the soil. We walk on stardust!

Soil is what allows all living beings, including trees, plants, and mammals like us, to have food to eat. When topsoil is healthy, water and air can easily move through it. About half the water in topsoil drains down through gravity. The other half is retained to hydrate and nourish plants and fill creeks during dry seasons. Without topsoil, we'd alternate between dry-pan droughts and flash floods. Think of the way asphalt and pavement covered cities flood during heavy rains and have heat shimmering off them in unbearable blasts when it is hot. I often marvel at how this does not happen in the ancient forest, where it stays relatively cool on warm days, and there is very little soil runoff during rains.

Add in the fact that in forests and grasslands three-quarters of total carbon storage is found in the soil and it's clear that soil is more precious than gold. As Furniss writes in his article:

Humans and humus and humility are all bound together in the same word, my friend. The dark productive earth is like your own vast interiority. Your inner life is as a soil. Dark, all productive, hard to see, immense, showing itself only in a penumbra of manifestation. Easy to forget and neglect, yet the source and substance of your life and creativity. Remember: You become soil when the time of your incarnation is done; human to humus. I (soil) give you birth, and wealth, and water. I give you plants and animals, and form the tissues of your history and sustenance. I am your outer and inner landscape, inside out and outside in, holding all. I am many more things, truly much more than you will ever need. Your bodies are just rearranged me. I am you.

I love this quote. It makes me tingle all over, expressing the way I feel about the beautiful, deep dark mystery of ourselves. We are each so much more than we know. There's both a glory and a humility in that. We are made of soil and we return to soil and that is the foundation of life. Sometimes the most precious aspects of ourselves and our world are also the ones we take the most for granted and neglect. Soil seems like one of those.

Thankfully, people are starting to do more to protect the soil. Los Angeles County has added compost bins along with recycling and trash for pickup. Instead of going to landfills where organic waste turns into methane gas, which exacerbates climate change, compost is taken for sorting and turned into nutrient-rich soil for farmers.

Lounging next to a giant redwood tree that is a short ten-minute stroll from the visitors' center, I still feel like I'm in another world. Leafy green alder and maple trees grow along a small creek, as well as huge old redwoods, which spire above me. I close my eyes for a moment of complete relaxation, allowing myself to feel the rich soil of the ground in the intact forest.

Forest Guidance

It's time to get dirty. Pot a plant in rich soil, walk barefoot and connect to Earth, dig your toes into the dirt. Spend five minutes doing nothing but looking at the soil. Once I sat at a redwood tree and watched a dung beetle roll a ball of dung, presumably intending to lay her eggs in the ball before burying it in the ground. It was actually rather fascinating. Later I discovered that a group of Swedish scientists led by Marie Dacke put little cardboard hats on the beetles' heads, blocking their view of the stars. The beetles became hopelessly lost. It turned out that they navigate by the Milky Way! The scarab, a symbol of rebirth in Egyptian mythology, was modeled after the dung beetle because of the way the young beetles emerge from the earth, new life rising. What bugs do you see? Are there earthworms, busy aerating the soil? Soil is foundational for our lives. Get your journal and write down all the foundational elements of your own life. What nourishes you? What brings you down to Earth and grounds you, making you feel fully present and right here? What is it you absolutely need to live and thrive?

18
Weather

*Working consciously with Earth, we navigate these
dynamic times of climate change in the easiest
and most gentle and graceful possible ways.*

By summer 2022, California had been in a severe drought for three years. Although the state has always experienced droughts interspersed with wetter times, the year 2022 saw the driest January, February, and March in one hundred years. I noticed this in the forest. Elk no longer grazed along the gravel bar. In a way this was a relief since I didn't have to worry about bucks blocking my trail and lowering their antlers at me, preventing me from getting back to my car. The herds were huddled closer to the coast, where it was damper and presumably they had an easier time finding green grass.

Toward the end of that summer, plants looked parched. I could almost hear trees screaming their thirst. Local people's wells were drying up, and some of them had to truck in water. Reservoirs across the state were so low that there was very little water storage. Could California even survive another drought year? Would people have water flowing from their faucets?

In the midst of that hot, dry time, I wrote in my journal: "It's so good to be out here, just not as good as I remember from sixty years of living in the glorious ecodiversity of California. Now there's high haze from fires in Yosemite, algae beginning even in the most pristine rivers, fewer fish, trees standing dead from sudden oak death, bark beetles, and rust fungus or toppling from the stress of drought—I read the worst in twelve hundred years. I bask in the beauty that is still here, waking to birdsong in a leafy green copse. I come to sleep close with the remaining wild, not knowing if these places I've loved all of my life and that have been here for millions of years will still be here next year. We've already lost places dear to me and many others to fires and they won't be restored in my lifetime. We live in such an elaborate, exquisite, delicate, complex, and interrelating biosphere. It's unimaginable to have life unraveling so quickly, literally before my eyes. My heart brings me back over and over again to be with nature every precious moment while this is still here. Whales and dolphins, egrets and owls, crawdads and steelheads. Scientists, mystics, Indigenous people, and the trees tell me that we still have a few years to turn this around and head toward thriving life."

Although we lost so many drought-weakened trees to the winter squalls of 2023, California and much of the West were saved by the wet winter and cooler temperatures. We were in a La Niña climate pattern, which happens when the surface temperatures of the ocean in the eastern tropical Pacific are unusually cold for at least a few months. It's normal for these years to alternate every two to seven years in an irregular cycle with the hotter El Niño weather. Sometimes there's even an in-between state where ocean temperatures are considered neutral, not too hot or too cold. Still, although La Niña can bring wetter weather to the Pacific Northwest, it usually brings drier-than-normal conditions to Southern and Central California. This didn't happen in 2023; all over California and the West, it was an extremely wet winter. The water was desperately needed, even if it did come down in such a harsh way.

Despite the cooling effects of La Niña, due to climate change,

2015 to 2022 have been globally the eight warmest years on record. However La Niña did temporarily slow down the rapidly rising global temperatures and give us a little breathing room to find ways to conserve water, choose to grow crops that need less water, and explore the possibilities of desalinization and how to deal with its side effects, like too much remnant salt potentially killing sea life. Although we made some headway, and people all across Southern California have been offered rebates to change their water-hogging front lawns to more drought-resistant plants, the warmer El Niño weather pattern will come again.

We are going to be living with a destabilized climate and more extreme weather events for a long time. Even writing these words makes me feel agitated. I wonder how you feel reading them. What changes are you noticing in your part of the world? While it is important to be aware of the challenges we face, perhaps there are solutions that we can't even imagine at this point. In the presence of the trees, visualizations arise of us working consciously with Earth to ameliorate some of the worst disasters.

Many times over the past fifteen years, I've had the same vision while sitting with ancient redwoods. The vision has come to me from Grandmother Dragon Tree in my backyard, Ancestor Tree, Summer Tree, and Star Tree. In it, I see a time where humanity is listening to Earth and following her guidance in restoring waterways, forests, and ecosystems of all sorts. We have come together all around the world and are cooperating to keep our precious planet habitable. Somehow Earth knows this. When I'm in the forest, my inner vision shows me people lit up: pink, green, gold, white, blue, and violet. We look like dancing lights or fireflies, all around the globe. Aware that we humans are doing our best and that most of our hearts' desires have changed from power and wealth as primary values to life, health, and beauty, Earth collaborates with us on restoration. In the vision, I see Earth soften the already built-in climate change blows. Perhaps hurricanes spend most of their force offshore, or storms dump the worst rains into the ocean instead of flooding towns and blowing away buildings. Fires are smaller and more contained. Gaia teaches us what to plant and where. Droughts are eased with gentle rains. Working consciously with Earth, we navigate these dynamic times of climate change in the easiest and most gentle and graceful ways possible. We know we are heading toward a beautiful grassy, green golden age. This could be.

Forest Guidance

Go to your special spot in nature and feel into your own vision of our world healed. What would it look like to you? What would you be doing differently? How might you, personally, partner with Earth? How would you feel doing this? Don't censor yourself: let your vision arise as it does—grand and expansive or small and intimate. After receiving the vision, think of one action that you can do to create the world your heart desires. Often we feel joyful when we are sharing our soul gifts.

All of us have soul gifts. When we realize and become conscious of our gifts and own them for ourselves, then it becomes possible to offer them to the world. Sometimes it can be hard to see our own gifts because we often take them for granted. They can be so natural to us that we don't realize they are gifts and assume everyone else has them. Sometimes we even mistake our gifts for faults.

Owning my gift of being able to put words to many experiences has allowed me to write books and sometimes help friends with verbal insights. Writing this book feels like a soul gift to me. Despite my worry and grief over fires raging close to some of my beloved redwoods this August of 2023, I feel a sort of creative ecstasy as I write and wonder if this could be the ebullient joy of the nature spirits finally getting to speak through me. If you feel drawn to do so, take a few moments to write what it is you have to share. Maybe even make a poem out of it.

19
A Fable for Our Times

*Earth Mother heard and she asked one of her beloved
forests, "People are waking up now. Do you think
they are ready for my miracles yet?"*

There came a time when it was clear things could not go on as they
had been. The people were hungry and clean water was becoming
harder and harder to find. But there were a few people, known as
gold counters, who liked the way things were. They were accumulating
lots and lots of gold. These gold counters could have anything they
wanted: toys, vehicles, five or six homes, and trips to exotic places—
maybe soon, even the moon or Mars. Every day, their stacks of gold
grew. They were so busy counting their gold that they did not notice
the weather. It was changing.

Cutting down forests and drilling Earth for her black blood had
earned the gold counters lots of gold, but it had also changed the
climate. In the West, fires raged. In the North, people froze. In the
East, there were floods. And in the South, fierce winds blew. People
were hungry and losing their homes. Animals were also hungry and
losing their homes. They tried to tell people this drilling and cutting
had to stop.

Whales called people with songs. Turtles came out from the
sea. Trees whispered loudly, inviting people to come close, listen, and

learn. Birds swooped down from the clouds. Gaia spoke in myriad ways, "Wake up! Wake up! Come home to me now!"

At first, not too many people heard. Most were busy working longer and longer hours for shelter and food.

But there were some who did hear: mystics and scientists found out that plants can feel, think, and speak. Whale singers and dolphin divers, bear dreamers and shamans, mothers and grandmothers, fathers and grandfathers, and children who wanted to grow up in a world with giraffes all heard and began to wake up.

People started to say, "Maybe we could live in a different way."

Friends and family asked each other, "What do we need to be healthy and happy?"

Voices chorused in conversations all over the world, "Clean water and air. Food and shelter. Beauty, nature, music, and art. Each other and the wildlife too."

The people stopped buying things they did not need.

The gold counters were not happy. Their stacks of gold were beginning to shrink. "We have to do something," said one man who, along with his eight friends, owned as much as half of the people on Earth combined. "We are losing money."

So they made big advertisements and put them on radio, TV, and billboards. "Consume! Buy more! It's a deal!"

But the people did not want their deal. With the money they'd saved by not buying things they did not need, they were planting trees.

"Let's buy the rights to all the fresh water," said the oldest gold counter.

"We'll profit on that," agreed the one with the beard.

"Oh no, you won't," said the people, and they sent the ones who knew the rule of law to speak in the courts of power so the water in holy springs, sacred wells, streams, and lakes would be protected for all.

The gold counters looked down at their dwindling piles of gold. "We will start another war," said the oldest gold counter. "That always boosts our wealth."

"Yes," said the one with the beard, "we'll tell the people how afraid they should be of the other people across the sea."

So they made big advertisements and put them on radio, TV, and billboards. "If we don't kill them, they will kill us," the gold counters said. "Send your sons and daughters to fight and we will give each one of them brand new boots and three meals a day."

This time the people weren't fooled. They'd gone outside and talked to the trees. They'd listened to birds and whales. They said, "No! We will not send our sons and daughters. Another war will not stop the fires, winds, or floods."

"But . . . but . . . but you need our war," spluttered the gold counters, "and you need to buy our stuff."

The people shook their heads. They laughed. "We know what we need now," they said. "Clean water and air. Food and shelter. Beauty, nature, music, and art. Each other and the wildlife too. When you're done counting gold, please come join us."

The people went outside, linking their hearts full of love in a wave of light that traveled the world. They all rose up together and said, "We have one precious planet. We need to care for Earth."

Earth Mother heard, and she asked one of her beloved forests, "People are waking up now. Do you think they are ready for my miracles yet?"

"Yes," said the forest, "they are planting more trees."

Where a few trees were planted, whole forests sprang up. Birds, animals, and fish came back. Woodlands changed the climate, bringing more rain. Springs and wells filled with fresh water.

Earth Mother smiled. "And now it begins."

Forest Guidance

My picture book *The Miracle Forest* tells the true story of a miracle that is happening right now. Paolo Lugari founded the sustainable community of Gaviotas in the barren savannas of eastern Colombia. At first, they couldn't get anything to grow in the acidic soil. Eventually, the community tried tropical Caribbean pines. The tropical pines survived and even supported the community by producing rosin they could sell.

Then the miracle happened: shaded in the understory of the pines, rainforest not seen in thousands of years spontaneously returned, bringing back over 260 species of flora and fauna as well as encouraging more rainfall. Trees draw moisture in through their roots and then release any extra moisture they do not use through leaves and needles. This water vapor forms into clouds that become rain, filling aquifers and springs. Biologists believe the forest regenerated either from dormant seeds in the ground, the droppings of passing birds, or both. This is a living example of the way, when we do our best, the intelligence of Earth can create miracles beyond our wildest dreams.

Paolo says that human artistic and creative expression is essential to creating the world we want. In their community center, the people of Gaviotas had a mural painted of all their dreams for the community. Everything depicted on the mural, including the air ship to watch for forest fires, has now come true. In the center of the mural is a banner that translated from Spanish says, "Maturity consists of making dreams come true." Take a moment to imagine the miracles of restoration you'd like to witness. Write, draw, paint, dance, sing, or use any other creative medium to tell the story of how it worked out and life on Earth survived the changing climate and is once again thriving.

20
Sitting with Sitka Spruce

When we root firmly into our own individual natures,
which are part of nature, we open a portal to connect
with the larger intelligences of wild nature: trees,
rocks, rivers, birds, bees, flowers, and even stars.

Stormy weather has had me going to a state park closer to home where I've been sitting in a grove of Sitka spruce trees on the cliffs by the sea. There's a yellow school bus in the parking lot, and I watch a group of children heading down to the beach. They look excited, laughing and chatting—animated. I'm glad to see them outside knowing how important nature education is for children. The word *education* stems from the Latin root *educare*, which means "to bring out or lead forth." I love the idea of children being led out into the larger world of nature, where the desire to learn and find out more about starfish and sea urchins, shells and agates is as innate as breathing. One beautiful example is Archangel Ancient Tree Archive's tree school, where children are taught to clone, plant, and care for trees so that the young people and trees literally grow up together.

Heading the other direction from the kids, I walk along a path, listening to ocean waves lap the shore, passing shade-loving green hosta plants, miner's lettuce with pink flowers, and small white daisies. Below is a herd, sometimes called a raft, of very noisy sea lions. One sounds like a hound dog wailing, another coughs *ugh, ugh, ugh*, and many bark exactly like dogs, *rrf, rrf, rrf*. If I get my binoculars out, I can make out the small flaps they have for outer ears. That's one way to tell them apart from the quieter, softly grunting harbor seals who are in the next cove over. Seals and sea lions are both pinnipeds, a word that derives from the Latin words *pinna*, which means "fin," and *pedis*, which means "foot."

Far out to sea, I see a spout that could be from one of the migrating gray whales. In spring, they return from their breeding areas in Baja California and head back up to the Bering Sea, where they can eat their fill of crustaceans and other creatures found in the ocean floor sediments.

Pelicans swoop and fly together in graceful lines as I make my way past a stand of white barked alder trees and draw closer to a Sitka spruce grove. Perched on the cliff above the rocky shoreline, the trees in this grove feel like sisters. Ravens fly by, kraaing loudly, surf beats the shore, wind lashes branches so they thrash and creak, and sea lions continue their bark-singing. There's so much going on that I find it hard to calm down and sink into the peace and quiet that I experience in the stillness of redwoods. Every type of tree and forest invites us into a different state of consciousness.

Here the refreshing, uplifting, almost effervescent quality of the trees literally spruces me up. It's more exposed than the deep, dark yin feeling of being immersed in the redwood forest. The spruce trees aren't so tall, and it is less shady underneath them. Fresh sea air blows my hair into tangles, and I feel mentally scattered about everywhere, part of me worried about my granddaughter, who has a respiratory virus, which could be COVID, other parts receiving ideas to write, and part thinking about what I'm going to make for dinner.

It's time to call myself home. I ask and visualize that all the essential bits and pieces of vibrating light that make up the field that is my essence return to my body, being and aura in their purest form. Feeling full from the sparkling energy coming into me, I also ask that anything I've picked up that is not me or in my highest and best interests be released, dissolved, evaporated, composted, or taken off with the angels. What a relief.

Now I feel more gathered together. Sitting for a long time, I open to this grove of spruce. Although this park is popular, no one ever comes to this out-of-the-way stand of trees. The Sitka spruce sisters seem to chatter together. I hear their tree music in my mind. Several times recently I've listened to machines hooked up to plants and trees that translate their electronic signals into music we can hear. Jesse, a member of the Archangel Ancient Tree Archive team, told me that the baby redwoods in their nursery make different music depending upon who walks into the room. Recently, I was given a recording of the tree music translated to piano. Steve, Allegra, and I were all flabbergasted because it sounded just like the piano music I improvise when I'm channeling the forest! Feedback like this makes me think I am actually hearing the trees serenading in my head right now, even without the electronic translation device.

The music is light and airy and sounds almost like laughter. Tinkling. Chimes and bells. Gongs. Crystal bowls. Slow pauses between notes, and then little flurries like flitting butterflies. These trees seem to know each other well, and their harmonies are effortless. I love this land where I live.

I'm bonded in an almost territorial way to the mountains to the east and to the many rivers, lagoons, bays, beaches, and forests of redwoods, spruce, and fir. It's like I have psychic roots sucking up nourishment; much of my well-being and strength comes from nature support. With so many varied ecosystems within a couple hours' drive, I am never bored. Actually, it's hard to pry me out of Northern California.

Many of us live rootless lives in the United States. For work, people often have to move far away from family and the communities where they grew up. Sending children off to distant colleges is so common that we have a term for the grief parents feel, *empty nest syndrome.* In a way, we miss the harvest of our grown and strong children living close by. When we no longer feel rooted to a particular location and community, we are less likely to protect it. We may not care as much about the removal of a random pine tree as we would if it was the pine we climbed as a child.

Even in our modern lifestyle, where many of us tumbleweed around, we can bond deeply with the land where we are. Time in the wild woods has helped me to do so. Returning again and again to the same places and trees, I've gotten to know them in many moods and weathers. I know where the sweet bubbling spring is. I know when and where the mariposa lilies bloom. This deeper relationship with place has healed me. Returning repeatedly to the same forest spot is actually a forest-bathing technique. We develop an intimate relationship. Familiarity allows our bodies to relax more deeply.

When I'm alone and quiet, I am more easily able to sense my body in relationship to the environment around me. I am much more aware of my surroundings. It is from this awareness that we are able to commune deeply with nature. When we root firmly into our own individual natures, which are part of nature, we open a portal to connect with the larger intelligences of nature: trees, rocks, rivers, birds, bees, flowers, and even stars.

This land I have been transplanted to has given me so much. I'm constantly fed the support of beauty, solitude, serenity, and love for the ground beneath my feet. Somehow, I've grown roots.

Legends claim that Mount Shasta is part of fabled Lemuria. Lemuria was supposed to be a peaceful place, sort of like a Garden of Eden, comprised of a large land mass that later became islands across the Pacific Ocean, including Hawaii. Oral stories passed down in Polynesia say a giant wave destroyed the land and Lemuria sank into the sea. This is similar to stories about Atlantis, although that land mass was said to be in the Atlantic Ocean instead of the Pacific.

Whether or not Lemuria ever actually existed, I love the story. For years, while sitting near trees, I'd hear a voice in my mind say, "You're from Mu." Moo? Like the sound a cow makes? I had no idea what that was, until eventually I discovered it is sometimes used interchangeably as another name for Lemuria. I picture myself in that legendary place, walking through leafy green foliage with a bird on my shoulder and flowers blooming at my feet. In the visions, I know I'm telepathic and can understand birds and animals as well as people. We Lemurians work with musical sounds to co-create reality along with the nature spirits.

Like the musical sounds of these Sitka spruce now, I hum along, adding my voice to the melody. Singing opens me up to my mystical right brain, and soon I'm in the enchanted realm.

Within the atmosphere of beautiful forests, I sometimes imagine myself as Lady Galadriel, Queen of the Elves from Tolkien's trilogy. As Lady Galadriel I step lightly, my feet barely touching the needles and leaves scattered across the forest floor. I sip from the wellspring of holy water, my cup a chalice of divine nectar. Feeling more alive, my hands take on a translucent glow. As my vibration rises further, I begin to perceive nature spirits.

Little flashes of colored lights weave themselves through the trees, adding their chiming voices to the medley. Dazzling yellow, blue, peach, fuchsia, and silver sparkle. Wherever the fairy lights touch, the green glows greener, and I can almost hear plants grow, bursting with vigor and life-force energy.

Merrily, merrily the nature devas do their creative work, stimulating growth, health, and life. "Help us with your song," sings a green fairy. "You are from the dolphin star," adds the silver fairy. "Sing along with us," chimes in the yellow fairy. "Find your own heart song, that's the way," says the pink fairy.

Putting my hands on my chest and allowing myself to root deeply into the Sitka spruce grove, my consciousness settles into the inner chambers of my heart. I add my voice to the ones I hear in my head. "La, la-la-la," I sing, thinking that maybe we can sing ourselves into a healed and regreened world.

Forest Guidance

Do you want to play with the elementals and dance with the fairies? Loosening our grip on what we know is real, we can soften into what might be. This can open us up to more subtle perceptions. When I do this, the sounds of the natural environment become more vivid. I listen with my heart and hear a nonphysical hum in the forest. Often other people tell me they also hear this hum. We live within the mystery of life. It is fun to let ourselves explore with childlike wonder. Occasionally what we perceive in that fantasy way overlaps into our lives with undeniable reality. Perhaps we feel more zing and zest and find ourselves singing to our houseplants, and suddenly they have a growth spurt and shoot up with glossy green leaves as mine did, or our skin takes on a healthy glow and we find ourselves laughing more.

21
The Golden Mead

Coming to wild places helps us access the golden mead
brewing deep within our souls.

In the Awakening Woman Freyja Sadhana, I learned about a special drink, a golden mead, found in Norse myths. Sometimes the mead was made from honey and associated with magical powers and long life. Our idea of a honeymoon comes from beliefs about the ability of this drink to enhance fertility. Sometimes, instead of a drink, the mead was poetry hidden in the underworld by the lady of wisdom.

The goddess Freyja is a guardian of the golden mead. People who drink this mead become *skalds* (scholars). When the mead was plentiful, it was a time of peace known as *frodafridr*. At that time, the wisdom of the gods was said to be available throughout the worlds, and it was a golden age.

Many of us now seeking to create a new golden age can look back at these myths and tease out the embedded hidden clues that might reveal a path to follow. Clearly, poetry must be part of this path, judging by the extremely important place myths like the one about Freyja give to poetry, hiding this treasure in the underworld. For me, poetry along with music and art is one way the gods talk to us; it is a way we can talk to the gods and to all of creation. Writing poems is different than prose in that words often arrive in flashes of inspiration, including an altered state of consciousness. We give breath and words to something larger than ourselves, something our language gently points toward, something we look at slantwise, glimpsing it from the corners of our eyes.

Coming to wild places helps us access the golden mead brewing deep within our souls. Nature has inspired numerous poets, including Robert Frost, Wendell Berry, David Whyte, and Mary Oliver. Poets like these have found the golden mead in their souls and brought it back to share with all of us. Perhaps it is because being in nature settles us. We are like a turbid stream after a storm, and nature sinks the floating debris in our minds. The waters of our being become clear, and we find the holy wellsprings within ourselves.

In the forest, I am able to let go of repetitive thoughts ranging from the endless to-do lists to replaying situations I wish I'd handled better. Sometimes stuck emotions come up, and I release places of hurt and locked-in-the-body old pain. Sitting in the comforting presence of Summer Tree, tears have rolled down my cheeks without my ever figuring out exactly what they were about. It hasn't felt necessary to go into the old stories. Instead, old hurts flow through my body and are washed clean with my tears. Afterward, I feel clear. That's when I am able to drink deeply from the golden mead.

One wound that came up was the one with other women. During the thousands of years of patriarchy, the individual survival of women has been inextricably linked to finding protection from a strong and hopefully kind man. This is still true in parts of the world where girls are not allowed to be educated and women are not allowed to work outside the home.

This need for a male protector set women up as rivals. Women certainly would have needed a powerful male protector during the European witch hunts, which lasted for an estimated and staggering three hundred years, from around 1450 to 1750. Women were accused of being witches for using herbs, practicing midwifery, or having property coveted by a neighbor. The underlying reason was that women were probably being scapegoated due to the environmental disaster of the Little Ice Age, when so many crops were lost, which Wolfgang Behringer covers in his book *A Cultural History of Climate*. People were looking for someone to blame. Sadly, it was frequently women and girls, probably trying to protect themselves or curry favor with powerful men, who were the ones accusing other women of being witches. Given this distressing history, it's easy to understand how strained relationships between women might become.

Cali White, an ancestral healing practitioner and psychosynthesis counselor, has done a lot of work to heal this "witch wound" and offers workshops and one-on-one healing sessions.* From 2020 to 2021, White gathered together and led thirty-three women to work on healing from the witch hunts, which have left a collective wound of inherited trauma that continues to shadow us. They named themselves the Silver Spoons Collective and in 2022 presented an educational and experiential exhibition they created called "I Am Witch: Tales from the Roundhouse," in Lancaster, UK.

This inherited trauma from the witch hunts expresses itself in me as distrust of other women. Worried I will make another woman jealous, in the past I have been reluctant to share good news or my strengths. I've presented myself wound first, telling other women everything wrong with me right off the bat to prevent the possibility of making anyone jealous. I didn't ask for much or expect "sistering."

That was before I connected with TreeSisters, a social change and reforestation charity based in Bristol, UK. Not only does this organization fundraise and donate money to plant trees, the members of TreeSisters also visualize themselves as a forest floor of women con-

---

*You can hear an interview of Cali White by Will Gehin on his podcast *Follow Your Blissters: The Hero's Journey*, series 2, episode 4, September 10, 2022.

nected by a mycelial root system. The image caught many women's fancy, as our relationships among ourselves were like the fungi in the forest transmitting chemical requests for and offers of nutrients among various trees. We asked one another for what we needed and generously offered what we had to give.

This is a beautiful model of how we can all heal—both women and men—from the patriarchal disruption to the community of women. Men have been harmed too by this competitive warrior model, which has entailed the loss of the sacred masculine. Instead of competing with one another, there is room for all of us to shine and offer our gifts. Like nature, which scientists have recently discovered depends much more upon cooperation than the old Darwinian "survival of the fittest" paradigm, we can help one another with networks of supportive relationships.

It's an odd juxtaposition, living in a time of crumbling old systems that are not conducive to our species and many others' survival, while at the same time striving to create something new out of the rubble. We need a little magic. And that's where forests come in, with their ancient breathing-healing magic. Here we can more easily find the golden mead of our souls.

Trees whisper in the wind. Something white hides behind one of the redwoods. Stepping softly, I tiptoe closer. The sound of my footfalls is muffled by the thick duff. What was that glimpse of white? Is that a luminescent horn? Peeking behind the tree, I imagine, sort-of see, an ethereal unicorn flickering in and out of sight.

"What are you doing here?" I murmur.

"You asked for magic," she speaks in my mind. Her words feel like ebullient bubbles expanding and dissolving.

I nod, wondering what magic the unicorn has to offer.

She answers my unspoken question. "I'm elusive and hidden. The pure in heart may find me in my forest havens. I offer the magic of innocence and hope. I offer the magic of finding what cannot be found and seeing what is here but not here."

Like with me right now. I know this unicorn is not really here. But something sweet is. Something that makes my skin have goosebumps is in the forest with me. An elegant grace.

"You remind me of trilliums," I say.

"We are related," the white horse with the singular horn agrees.

"Are you a fantasy?" I ask.

The unicorn snorts. "I exist in parallel higher dimensions of light. Fairies travel on my back between worlds."

"They do?" I ask, wishing I could stroke her lustrous mane.

"You can," she says. "Come closer."

I move beside her glistening light body and reach a tentative finger up to her sleek mane. My hand sparks, the way it does with static electricity. There is something here!

She paws the ground. "I'm here. I came to help you connect to the elemental and angelic spheres. We will do this through your own childlike innocence." Playing here with an imaginary unicorn does feel pretty childlike.

"OK," I say.

"I've been with you for decades, helping you to heal your inner child."

"Thank you," I reply, thinking that I've spent much of my life healing self-worth and self-esteem issues, as well as limiting inherited beliefs and toxic cultural messages.

She kneels down in the redwood sorrel beside a gnarly old tree. Sitting beside the unicorn a few feet from the trunk, I luxuriate in the radiant field of the old tree.

"You knew me in Lemuria." Her gentle thought floats into my mind.

"Lemuria is real?"

"As real as your imagination. Image-in the world you want. In

Lemuria, you were a light being like me, delicate and interdimensional. There was no sickness, and you lived for thousands of years, like these old trees. The trees remember Lemuria. That's why it's easier for you to remember Lemuria when you are with them."

I close my eyes and feel something hard lightly tap on my third eye, my sixth chakra. Perhaps it is the unicorn horn. Opening my eyes again, the world looks different. Everything around me flickers and shimmers, and I can see through the tree. I see atoms or maybe molecules, small particles oscillating as if the forest is breathing with me.

"Now you're here," says the unicorn, sounding satisfied. "Welcome to the mystical realms."

How could the colors be this bright? I want to leap and prance and spin about with the delight of being alive.

"Please share stories of us," says the unicorn. "It's important people don't forget." Her voice in my mind fades, and soon I can no longer see the slightly wavy distortions in the air, like a heat mirage, where I imagined she was.

Why is it so important that people don't forget a creature out of fantasy? I get up to walk back on the twilight trail to my car. Is it the state of being we need to not forget? The childlike joy and innocence of our spirits? The mythic imagination and creativity that have been cross-cultural road maps around the world? Is this part of the golden mead of our souls?

Forest Guidance

Where do you open to the magic of life and find the golden mead? Is there a poem or piece of music that speaks to you? What fills your cup to brimming and overflowing? Does one particular landscape inspire you? Think of a time when you felt your absolute best. Perhaps the colors looked brighter, the water tasted so delicious that you couldn't believe it was simple water, or the sparkle in a partner's eyes made your heart leap. Record or take a moment to write as fast as you can for five straight minutes without stopping, "The golden mead for me is . . ." Begin each sentence with this phrase. Don't try to think up the answer. Let it flow right out of your mouth or pen completely uncensored. When you have all your phrases together, pour a glass of water and imagine it is your chalice. Play your recorded words or read all of your phrases aloud over the cup. Sip this water slowly, knowing you are imbibing the holy water of your own golden mead, and it is bringing more of everything you named into your life.

22
Unicorn Magic

Feel the star song in your soul.

*I*maginal is a word that means "relating to images, dream characters, stories, and imagination." I first heard it when I was participating in a class called "Birth of a Poet" at UC Santa Cruz and we were studying Jungian dreamwork. The word *imaginal* captured my own imagination because it is active. Something wouldn't be "just my imagination." Instead, it was an ongoing, imaginal experience. I've been playing with these states of consciousness ever since, allowing myself to go beyond the borders of my rational mind the same way we do in our dreams at night. Even waking, we can temporarily suspend the dominating disbelief of the intellect and allow ourselves to expand into the imaginal realm, a place where dreams are conceived. It is from here, in the imaginal realm, that the unicorn speaks to me. She taps my forehead gently with her horn and then begins to speak.

We have one horn. We are one pointed, of one mind, one heart, and one body. We are all white, a color that reflects all other colors, glistening in our own truth and perfection. We exude the innocence of purity and the purity of innocence. We are childlike wonder and hope. We are invisible and all around. We are within you and without you. We are the unicorns of myth and fairytale, the ones you want to believe in and know are true on some metaphysical level.

Ride with us into the enchanted worlds. Feel the star song in your soul. Feel the enigmatic truth of the multidimensional reality that is constantly in flux, evolving, flowing, changing, one thing becoming another. Tree to soil to worm to mushroom to sprouting tree again. Feel your place in this vast universe of change.

We are here to guide you into what your hearts yearn for: beauty, peace, love, and contentment. Notice the pebble at your feet, an ordinary sandstone. It is striated with beautiful red designs. Beauty is everywhere. Treasure the small and ordinary.

Think of the sea cucumbers you see snorkeling. Brown, green speckled blobs not doing much of anything. There are over a thousand species of sea cucumbers. Seeming small and insignificant, sea cucumbers play a vital role in the health of your world. They scavenge the sea floor, digesting sand and mud and leaving calcium carbonate in their wake. This calcium is essential to the creation of the coral reefs, which support fish who then feed whales, dolphins, and birds, whose droppings fertilize your fields. Nothing is irrelevant in the great web of life. All has an important place, including you. Allow your own magic of self to shine. Until you own your gifts, you will not be able to share them. When you do own, honor, and acknowledge your gifts, the holographic-blueprint light codes to manifest them on Earth will pour into you. We unicorns work with angels and fairies to help you imbibe this celestial light.

Understand the transformational quality of life. Nothing stays the same. You are not the same you that you were a week, month, year, or decade ago. Morphing, changing, rearranging. This is the magic of life. Every drop of water in a river has been carried to the sea. Not a molecule of water is the same, and yet the river remains the same river. In this way, you are renewed and yet continue to have a recognizable quintessence, a "you" people know as you. But who are you? It's easier to discern when you slow down and care for yourself.

Care for yourself. Get the rest you need. Humans need sleep. It is when you are most able to contact us and travel to the renewing higher dimensions. If you can fall asleep by 10 p.m., most of you will experience deeper renewal. To make sleep come more easily, take warm salt baths, turn off screens a couple hours before bed, and spend some time every day outside in the sun. This will increase your feel-good hormones like serotonin and stimulate your pineal glands to release melatonin at night. If there is no sun, find a beautiful place and let beauty activate your pineal gland.

Eat foods with higher vibrations. Fruits and vegetables in particular will raise you up and alkalize your bodies. Think of the beautiful colors: blueberries, cherries, carrots, and oranges. Don't forget the herbs: green thyme and holy basil, chamomile and nettles. Herbs will support your body as you descend into the truth of your beings, and also as you ascend into more subtle frequencies, allowing latent potentials in humanity to be born. There are capacities in human beings that have not yet been turned on or activated.

Human capacities include qualities you've labeled as superpowers, like telepathy, unexplained knowing, being able to read objects and understand some of their history from holding them in your hands, communication with plants and animals, and manifesting on a scale that is currently unimaginable to you.

Stay open with the curiosity you had as a child. Don't assume you know everything. How could you?

Follow us deep into the forest of belonging. Let us whisper to you in the land of reverie, reminding you of your wholeness and love. Put the power of your focus and attention toward what you do want. While it is important to know what is going on, it is also important to protect what is precious. This is why we unicorns are seldom seen, elusive and hidden in the most holy old forests. We love yew trees as well as redwoods, oaks, and pines and are often glimpsed in these woodlands.

Your media is collectively focusing your attention on disasters, wars, catastrophes, profaned sexuality, and a host of horrors. When too many people hold these visions in their minds, they become more likely to manifest.

Allow yourselves to dream. What do you want? Take one small step in that direction. The garden grows one seed at a time. Follow our unicorn tracks deep into the unknown. Shhh. Shhh. Shhh. This must be done quietly. Tracks are hard to discern across the sands of time. Erased in false histories, you've forgotten that peace once existed and is possible again. Templates still remain in the nonphysical that are maps of peaceful coexistence. The universe knows harmony. All can be brought back into coherence. Even the sourest note can be part/of the beautiful symphony of life.

We unicorns have decided at this critical juncture in the history of humanity to make ourselves more available. Many of you will feel the light touch of our barely substantial effervescence, giving you hope where there was none, courage when you need it, heart when it is least expected. Pay attention to these whiffs of something better. It's yours for the asking.

Working with angels and fairies, we come to those in need. We come to artists and dreamers, poets and visionaries. We come to those who are hurt and those who are healing. We come to inspired scientists practicing open-minded observation. We come to mothers, fathers, and children, of course, and all of you who are innocent at heart.

The present moment is always the point of power. You are powerful when you are honest with yourself. Don't try to leap over how you actually feel. We angels, fairies, and unicorns respond to your complete broadcast anyway, and there's no faking that. Any feeling felt will transform into another one. Grief carves deeper pathways to love. Anger gives energy for action. Fear alerts you to what is wrong. All your feelings are gifts of love. Don't try to *suppress, ignore, or get over them. Get into your feelings. They are a high road into unicorn magic.*

Unicorns are the quintessential possibility of the mystical made real. Unicorns are your knowledge that something so beautiful and innocent and pure exists. We exist in your hearts. Wake up to the angels, fairies, and unicorns within you, and watch yourself grow. We are watching you with great tenderness and blessing.

Once again, the unicorn taps my forehead gently with her horn. I see myself as an irrepressible morning glory vine, blooming pink, blue, violet, and white. No matter how I've been trimmed and pruned back, told not to grow, been tamed and stunted, the vine of myself has found a way. Growing over, under, around, and through, I see improbable blossoms all around me.

Forest Guidance

Nature therapy often opens us up to nonordinary mind. We are no longer inside the rectangular shapes of many of our homes and buildings. There is no ceiling on our thoughts. Instead, we may find ourselves enjoying the deep, dark yin secret of the forest, the wide horizons of the desert or ocean, or the clear view of a mountain peak. Allow your chosen place in nature to help open you up to the imaginal realm. One fun way into this altered state of consciousness is to see the shapes in clouds. Is that a flying horse or a dragon in the sky? Or watch the ripples in the water form patterns. Notice the faces in boulders and on the trunks of trees. If you cannot get outside, stare at a picture of nature, listen to recordings of natural sounds, or find a guided visualization for an active imagination meditation.

23
Dryads

Many of us are now seeking ways to embody our
spirituality . . . here on Earth where we live.
We do not have to ascend to experience
our spirituality.

*H*ave you ever felt like you were becoming a tree? This happened to me once when I was about nineteen in Boulder, Colorado. I was sitting beside a giant old pine tree in the foothills of the Rocky Mountains. It was a cold day with patches of snow all about. Breathing, I fell into a sort of trance where I sensed myself merge with the tree. My seat and my feet seemed rooted into the ground, and my head felt like it elongated and poured my spirit into the tree, reaching up through her heartwood to branches stroking the sky. Despite the blustery day, it felt utterly blissful, and so I sat and sat for a couple hours.

Later, when I stood up, I realized that I couldn't feel my feet. My toes were numb. Growing up in Southern California, I didn't know much about frostbite. But when I took my boots off, I could see that my toes looked grayish-white. An older man who was a longtime resident of Colorado told me to soak my feet first in lukewarm water and then gradually warm the water until a nice healthy pink color returned to my toes.

I never forgot that feeling of almost becoming a tree. Maybe it is possible for human beings to merge their spirits with trees.

Like most cultures around the world, Greeks believed nature was alive with spirits. Nymphs, beautiful female nature goddesses, were found wherever there was fresh water, healthy animals, mountains, or trees. Nymphs were believed to be as infinite in number as the various places in nature. Dryads were the nymphs who inhabited trees. The dryads, along with most nymphs, were lesser goddesses. Although they did have some small powers, dryads were confined to one place on the physical Earth.

In Greek the word *drys* actually means "oak," and originally the term *dryad* referred specifically to those nature spirits who inhabited oak trees. Later the word included spirits from all sorts of trees in forests or woodlands, including ash, pine, poplar, apple, and laurel. Some, known as hamadryads, were so tied to the tree that when the tree died so did the dryad. Because the Greeks believed that cutting down a tree that sheltered a hamadryad would kill the nature spirit, doing so violated divine law and was considered to be murder. When trees needed to be pruned or harvested for fruit, ancient Greek people made offerings and thanked the tree dryads. In cases where the tree needed to be cut for some reason, they asked permission from the gods before proceeding.* I can't help wishing we could still see the spirits of trees this way, as holy and as deserving of life as we ourselves are.

Human beings weren't the only risk to the hamadryads. Natural disasters could also harm trees. Certainly we are seeing that now, with the loss of so many trees to fires, floods, hurricanes, and drought, along with invasive insects and pathogens. In Greek myth, Chrsopeleia was a dryad who lived in an oak that grew by a river. Her tree was in danger when the river flooded, and a hunter, Arcas, built a dam and rerouted the river to save her oak. Chrsopeleia was so grateful for his

---

*See Greenberg, "Dryads: The Nymphs of the Trees."

quick action that she fell in love with him and they had two children. He became King Arcas, the founder of Arcadia. I live in a town called Arcata, a name that probably derives from this myth.

Ancient Greek images carved in stone and wood show us dryads with hair-like leaves and moss-covered bodies peering at us through the trees. Looking at the redwood trees all around me in this forest, it is easy to see where these images may have come from. Often I perceive faces and figures on the trunks of trees: old men with beards, turtles, otters, and owls in the gnarls and burls. Sometimes they even seem to come alive, and I imagine their voices in my head.

The Greeks believed that people could find peace from sitting under a tree. They aren't the only ones who discovered this tranquility. As I've mentioned previously, the Japanese have proven with shinrin-yoku that we do calm down in the presence of forests, and there are all sorts of measurable and beneficial effects. I'm sure you will be able to experience this for yourself by going to a park or forest.

Forests are integral to a healthy environment. As many of us know, trees absorb the carbon that is a primary driver of climate change, as well as releasing the oxygen essential for our survival. They keep soil from eroding, cool the climate, create more water through transpiration, provide habitat for all sorts of birds, animals, and insects, are a source of inspiration and beauty, and even have a relationship with the life of whales. Orcas, a type of whale found swimming off the coast between California and British Columbia, depend upon salmon as an important food source, and the salmon depend upon healthy forests.*

Salmon begin in freshwater streams and rivers, and then swim down to the sea where there are more nutrients. They spend up to seven years in the ocean before it is time to spawn, and then swim back up to the place where they were born. I have witnessed salmon

---

*See Weeden, "Orcas, Salmon, and Trees: A Film & Conservation Initiative."

come to spawn and die in the creek behind my house. The way they thrash and fight their way upstream is impressive. After releasing their eggs in their birthplace, salmon die, and their bodies offer nutrients to the forest, including the nitrogen and phosphorus plants and trees need.

It's a mutually beneficial relationship, as the salmon also need the trees. The shade trees provide keeps the fish eggs cool. Falling leaves offer food for the insects that feed the young salmon. Roots stabilize the soil along the banks of creeks. Downed trees create dams where salmon swim in the deeper pools.*

I could go on. It turns out that whales also absorb huge amounts of carbon during their lives, and saving them is as important as saving forests. Ecological balance is maintained through the intricate inter-relationships of diverse life-forms. For the health of all of us, we need to knit the unraveling systems back together. And some of our inspiration to do so resides in a worldview that reveres nature as the Greeks revered the dryads, as intelligent, alive, and holy.

Whether or not people can actually see them, dryads were known to inspire human beings with feelings of wonder, awe, joy, and peace. Although dryads are shy and seldom seen, mythology has it that they did come out sometimes to dance. Perhaps the most famous dryad in Greek mythology is Daphne.

Daphne was a naiad. In Greek mythology, naiads or nymphs are female spirits who guard wells, creeks, springs, and fresh water wherever it is found. Clearly, the ancient Greeks understood the value of clean water. When Apollo lusted after Daphne and pursued her with unwanted sexual advances, she ran and prayed to Gaia for help. Before Apollo kissed her, Daphne called on Earth Mother, or in some versions her river god father, and she was transformed into a laurel tree. This myth depicts trees as refuge and shelter. Despite my fear of encounter-

---

*See Baron, "Salmon Trees"; and Post, "Why Fish Need Trees and Trees Need Fish."

ing mountain lions or bears, I do feel a sense of shelter, refuge, and safety when I am immersed in the forest.

This worldview of nature as sacred and inhabited by deities is a sort of animism I think we are getting back to as we heal the split between matter and spirit. The word *animism* comes from the Latin *anima*, which means "breath, spirit, life" and encompasses the belief that all people, plants, animals, and places, including rocks, rivers, mountains, and trees, have their own spiritual essences. It's a belief that can be found in the indigenous roots of almost every culture around the world.

Many of us are now seeking ways to embody our spirituality and bring it right home, here on Earth where we live. We do not have to ascend to experience our spirituality. There is no split between matter–Mother Earth and the divine. As Joni Mitchell put it in her song "Woodstock": "We are stardust, we are golden, and we've got to get ourselves back to the garden."

Seeing the sacred in all creation is one way back to the garden.

Forest Guidance

One way to let nature become more alive and to see the sacred in creation is to practice with a tree, rock, plant, flower, body of water, or animal. Imagine the being you are playing with as conscious, sacred, and intelligent. Pay attention to how your chosen nature being looks, smells, and feels, noticing details like texture, color, sound, and movement. Is this being smooth or rough? Warm or cool? Fast or slow? Going deeper into the experience, write or record: In your presence, I feel . . . Go on until you cannot think of any more feelings you have. If you are drawn to do so, imagine what it would be like to be this other being, as I did with the pine tree so long ago. How do you feel as a tree, standing still in one place for your whole life? What do you do when the weather is stormy and your branches lash and sway in the wind? Perhaps you are work-ing with a whale. Dive deep and then surface and let yourself spout off. Send your whale songs across the sea. Pretending to be another being is a great way to increase empathy and come closer to nature.

24
Sacred Sexuality

*My love affair with Earth is a journey into the erotic
and the sensual and a physical immersion,
which is the glory of nature's art.*

*T*he split humans have created between matter and spirit is at
the heart of our loss of sacred sexuality. Instead of the potential holy union sex provides, uniting our physical and energetic bodies, we've lost our way in a swamp of confusion. Sex has somehow
been degraded to a huge pornography industry as well as trafficking.
Worldwide, trafficking is the third-largest illegal industry, after drugs
and weapons. Many of those trafficked are children used as sexual
slaves.*

I can't even wrap my mind around the damaged and warped psychology that leads a person to get off on terrorizing and destroying
other people's well-being and innocence. However, these realities seem
at the center of our exploitive, distorted, and out-of-balance relationships with ourselves, one another, and Earth. My inner knowing tells
me that healing our sexuality is central to healing our relationship
with the loving, abundant, healthy, and unsuppressed eros of Earth.

---

*You can find information about the trafficking of children for sexual purposes at the
Monique Burr Foundation for Children: Prevention Education Programs and ECPAT
(End Child Prostitution and Trafficking).

We may be making some progress. I remember through junior high school and high school, boys slapping me on the butt and snapping my bra strap. This was something that occurred fairly regularly for many women of my generation, and it didn't even cross my mind to object. It was how things were and meant that the boys thought we were cute. But this kind of sexual objectification is a long way from the sacred sexuality Freyja seeks as she wanders the land, longing and looking for ecstatic union, crying golden and amber tears.

So many women I know are wandering the land, longing for a type of ecstatic union with a partner that seems rare and elusive. We somehow have an inchoate knowing that, as good as our sexual relations often are, there could be something more we are either missing or experience rarely. We sense a state of union with trust so exquisite that we can open wide to floating in the universal sea of bliss, until we are vessels overflowing with love, lighting up the world.

In her search, Freyja meets four dwarves. They have a necklace of protection and power to give her, called Brisingamen. In order to get the necklace, Freyja must go to the mountains and spend one night sleeping with each dwarf. Perhaps because she sleeps with all four dwarves, when Christianity came to the Norse lands, priests deemed Freyja promiscuous. However, there is another way to look at the myth. Sleeping with all four of them could be a metaphorical representation of her embodying all four of their qualities or truths. In the Norse myth, these are: spirit, essence, inspiration, and poetry. The four qualities are pillars to lean on and navigate sacred boundaries. Interesting that poetry comes up again as a foundation for a good life.

The four pillars can vary for each of us, depending upon what we most value. In my own life, my biggest values are: family, friends, being in wilderness, and creative expression. Knowing this helps me, as there are so many places I can put my energy and often I can't keep up with all of them.

Like Freyja, I search for ecstatic union with my husband. Steve and I have been together for forty-three years now. That could be boring. We don't get that heady falling-in-love feeling. I sense that we all love that state of new love so much because it allows us to project our fantasy images onto the other person. We imagine them as the god or goddess, the beautiful other half of our yearnings. We project our own light and goodness onto them. And then we are later disillusioned and disappointed when the person turns into another flawed human being.

As Steve and I bumble through the ups and downs of life together, I'm glad to have one long-term partner. I'm easily overstimulated, and the excitement of new love is far less attractive than the trust, comfort, and simple peace of being with one person. There's enough variety for me in the organic changes of life. No person is ever exactly the same; we are in constant flux, responding to arising conditions. Love changes and grows over time. It's easy to see with our children: we love newborn babies, are enchanted at the same child's three-year-old antics, and stay up way too late at night to be sure our newly driving teenagers make it home safely. Steve and I are like those rivers I mentioned previously, the same and yet not the same. So, in a way, I'm always falling in love with someone new.

And there are those times where we do break through to the numinous. Moments where for some mystical reason we crack open, and physical union is a union of souls that unites us with the greater All-That-Is. I have a sense of the infinite possibilities and also of the way this sort of coming together feeds Earth. It's the micro of the cosmic love affair between Earth and sky.

Our sexual connection deepened over my years of finding my own wholeness in the forest. The balance of spending time alone and then coming together is part of sacred sexuality. If we don't have enough time to fall in love with ourselves, then we can't bring this level of self-acceptance and well-being to the relationship. Freyja wanders the land alone looking for union. And she does unite with the four disparate parts of herself, finding her own completeness. It is this fullness, this quality of integrated self that leads us to healthier relationships with each other and the land.

My love affair with Earth is a journey into the erotic and the sensual and a physical immersion, which is the glory of nature's art. There's a sense of belonging, of being part of a multidimensional forest organism that is so much bigger than myself. I can hear the note of my own song, smell the fragrance that is mine alone, mingling with that of tree resin and spicy plants. Without interacting with another person's energy, I become intact and able to discover myself. Time in the trees allows me to feel into my core. I now believe that the core of all of ourselves is beauty incarnate. We are part of the divine expressing as life.

When we bring this wholeness to our sensual unions, it is no longer two hungry ghosts grasping, clinging, and desperately seeking. Instead, women can be like the fallow land, open, receptive, allowing ourselves to be seeded with regenerative love.

Culturally, most of us have lost something precious. But Earth still knows. Time alone in nature can be our teacher. What if making love is a way to fertilize our souls and bring healing back to the land?

Forest Guidance

Go to your quiet place outside. I've chosen a forest, but the following exercise can be adapted to practice anywhere in nature. Find a place where you will not be disturbed. Take your shoes off. Allow the softness of moss, the prickle of needles, or the coolness of mud to inform you through the soles of your feet. How do your toes feel against the ground? Notice the air. Is it warm, moist, or fragrant? Drink in the sensations from the air on your skin. Gently hug the tree. Wrap your arms around her. Is her bark rough or smooth? Warm or cool? Feel your heartbeat against the trunk as you allow your body to melt into the tree, naturally synchronizing with the subtle internal rhythms of her sap flowing through the heartwood. Inhale deeply, becoming aware of her fragrance. Is it spicy, warm, sweet, or earthy? Listen to leaves or needles swaying in the breeze, chipmunks and birds, or the soft hush of the deep forest.

Get into the most comfortable position you can, sitting or lying down. Stroke your own hair, face, neck, arms, and shoulders, down to your feet, touching and waking up your body to more conscious sensation. Allow the erotic sensuality of nature to envelop you as you open all your senses. When it is time to come back, be sure to ground yourself and take some time to integrate the experience of sensually opening up to nature. Perhaps take a few moments to write in a journal, record in your phone, or draw a picture. Drink some water or have a tea ceremony, as traditional shinrin-yoku forest bathers often do. The more time we take to integrate our experiences, the more long-lasting benefits we may experience.

25
Rutting Elk

Roosevelt elk can weigh as much as
twelve hundred pounds.

For elk, sex is a community event. I've run into herds of them during rutting season, which begins in late August and lasts until early October. They won't let me pass. Bulls guard those actually mating. The female cows are grouped into the center in harems. When I've walked up to them on the trail, the bulls lower their antlers, stomp their feet, and have even bugled, threatening to charge in attempts to scare me off. It works great. Roosevelt elk can weigh as much as twelve hundred pounds and seem huge when I'm on foot near them. No way am I passing a group of rutting elk. One time, Allegra and I were at the end of a long, eight-mile hike when we ran into the herd of elk.

A bull elk spots us hiking down the flat, coastal trail sandwiched between steep, forested cliffs on one side and marshy lagoons on the other. He bugles a warning. It's a loud clarion call, trumpeting out into the day. Answering the call, an even bigger elk dashes up and lowers his enormous antlers.

Allegra and I back off, never taking our eyes off the threatening elk. Instead of leaving us alone, the elk follows, steering us away from the cows. After a while, the elk stops and watches as we continue to back away.

Since the herd is between us and our car, half a mile away, we need to get by. Soon. The sky is already dusky with early evening light. When we are finally far enough away from the bull elk, I suggest, "Let's wade through the marsh and skirt around the herd down the beach."

"Good idea," replies Allegra, unlacing her boots. "It looks shallow."

"Yeah," I agree somewhat unenthusiastically. The wetland between us and the ocean also looks slimy. Taking off my shoes, I step into the squishy mud.

"Oh my God!" exclaims Allegra, pointing at the elk. "He's following us again!"

"Yikes!" Holding my shoes, I leap out of the bog and run barefoot through the soft grass back toward the path.

Pacing behind us, the elk follows, keeping a steady thirty feet between us. Elk can move fast, and I know he could be on us in an instant. The bull elk lowers his antlers menacingly. "He's going to charge!" screams Allegra.

We're totally exposed in the dunes. There isn't a tree, bush, or even driftwood to hide behind.

We run as fast as we can.

The bull elk doesn't charge, but he stays right behind me and Allegra, shepherding us all the way back up to the trail that ascends the cliffs into the forest before stopping and watching as we hurry up a couple of switchbacks. We shove our shoes back on our sore and bruised feet and watch as the elk finally turns and ambles back to the herd. Panting to catch my breath, I say, "What an alpha elk."

"Probably his first time on the job," agrees Allegra.

I sigh. "We're going to have to hike back on the loop."

Allegra groans. "Seven miles up and down hills. We'll never make it before dark."

"Maybe if we keep running," I suggest, and the adrenaline coursing through our bodies helps us jog up the cliffs, passing creeks bordered by giant alders until we enter the Sitka spruce and Douglas fir forest. I shoot off texts to my daughter and Steve, telling them where we are, but service out here is sketchy and I'm not sure they went through.

Sweating, we make it about four miles before it becomes too dark to see. Digging in my pack for my small hiking flashlight, I realize it is not there. I felt so safe having a friend with me that I took out the first-aid kit, which included my light, in order to make room for our rather large picnic lunch. Taking out my phone, we use the built-in flashlight to continue walking carefully over protruding roots. When the battery dies, I take out my UV water filter, and we continued to stumble along in its dim light.

We are still two miles away from the parking lot when even that feeble light gives out. "That's it," I say. "This trail is too dangerous to hike in the dark."

We sit down and lean back against a fallen log covered in thick moss.

"Will Steve come get us?" Allegra asks hopefully.

"Eventually. He knows which trail we are on. But he won't worry until an hour after dark, and then it's an hour drive. They lock the gate to the parking lot after dark too, so he will have to walk in two extra miles. Plus he will assume that we are coming home on the coastal trail the way we always do, so he will probably go that way first. I doubt he will be here until the wee hours of the morning."

"Oh," says Allegra, and there is a whole world of disappointment in that one word.

Chilly in my sweaty clothes, I notice there isn't much water in my canteen and barely a few scraps of food left over from lunch.

"Let's meditate. We don't have anything else to do. Maybe we will get enlightened tonight," I joke.

"OK," replies Allegra. "We need to calm down."

We shut our eyes and listen to the quiet hoots of night birds. Suddenly, the noises seem louder. There's a creak and crackle from the nearby bushes. Then a scrunch-crunch munching sort of sound. Our eyes pop open. "It could be a bear!" exclaims Allegra.

My whole body is tense and alert. "Or a lion. They come out at night."

"If we are too quiet, the animals might trip on us in the dark," worries Allegra.

"Right," I agree, thinking that bobcats, bears, and lions also prefer to use the trails. "We're going to have to make noise."

We take turns singing until our throats feel raw. Then we clap, clack our poles, kick our feet, and snap our fingers. It's only been a couple hours, and I'm already exhausted. "I can't keep this up," I say. "How are we going to talk and make noise all night?"

Allegra and I sit silently for a while. Then we hear something stirring behind the towering trees. I clap a couple of times, and the rustling stops. It was probably a chipmunk, but I feel totally unnerved. The rising moon casts silvery light through the trees. "Too bad it's not full tonight," I say hoarsely. "It won't be enough to see the path."

Allegra sighs. "It's going to be a long night."

I squirm around, trying to find a comfortable position on the ground. The trail is between a steep ravine on the eastern side and a tree-covered slope on the other side. "Let's take turns telling stories."

Allegra begins, "Once upon a time there was a fairy and an elf, and they were stranded in a dark forest in the middle of the night . . ."

My ears strain to hear every little noise, and I'm actually too freaked out to close my eyes for long, so both our eyes are wide open when we see little fairy lights dancing up the trail. "Do you see those?" whispers Allegra.

"Yes," I answer, wondering if this is another mystical experience. The lights bob around, up and down, circling in patterns. They become larger and larger. There are three lights. I hear footsteps. Then loud breath. A shadow looms out of the darkness. Two legs, a head, arms . . . "Steve?"

"There you are," he answers, handing each one of us a flashlight. "What happened?"

Allegra and I talk at once, telling him about the rutting elk.

Steve listens and then asks, "Why didn't you bring your flashlight?"

Hanging my head, I admit, "I took it out of my daypack to fit in more lunch."

Steve shakes his head, and I can tell he is a bit annoyed having to rescue us at midnight on a Saturday night.

But Allegra and I are ecstatic. We are rescued.

Next time, I will bring my flashlight.

Forest Guidance

To enjoy a positive forest-bathing experience, it is important to bring the right equipment. First is a good pair of walking shoes. Wear comfortable clothes with layers for changing weather conditions. Don't forget something to sit on. I usually carry a sarong in my daypack. They are light, dry quickly, and can provide shade, a wrap dress after a swim, and something to recline upon. Water in a canteen, a paper and pen to write ideas and inspirations, basic first aid if roaming far from the car, binoculars, and snacks are other things to consider. And don't forget a small flashlight! Some people may want bug spray, depending upon the area. I've found citronella and some of the other natural sprays have kept the mosquitoes away. If you aren't hiking far, a yoga mat or pillow can be welcome. And, if you are going alone, as I sometimes love to do, be sure someone knows when to expect you home, exactly where you are, including which trail—and stay on that trail!

26
Exuberance

*There's a playful side of myself that feels free
to come out in the woods.*

It's May now, and my birthday today as I write this. Yesterday, to celebrate, my daughter Michelle and Steve went to one of my favorite groves with me. It was a damp day, but we still enjoyed the peaceful feeling in the trees. Michelle made an incredible lunch, and we sat by the full flowing river, eating her delicious banana bread, sandwiches, and tangerines. We watched an osprey swoop over the gray-green river.

Eventually, I went up to meditate by Star Tree, and she and Steve took a nap in the sand by the beach. Michelle dreamed she was home on her BioMat (an infrared heating pad), woke up and realized she was chilled, so we headed back up the trail. Songbirds were back and singing. The forest looked ravaged with downed trees. More than I'd ever seen come down all at once. But there were enough old redwoods, bigleaf maples, alders, and California bay laurels standing that the grove still felt like an enchanted place.

And the moss was incredible. Epiphytic moss dangled eerily from tree branches. Thick velvety, vibrant green moss coated fallen logs and stumps. Moss is one of the oldest plants, dating back 450 million years, and has survived all sorts of changes in climate. According to Robin Wall Kimmerer in her book *Gathering Moss*, there are over twenty thousand species of moss, and they are found on every continent. One of the first plants to grow in areas that have been disturbed by fires or, in this case, high winds, mosses help the soil retain water so new plants can grow. Like snow on the ground, they seem to soften everything in the forest and make it look enchanted.

Mosses do not have roots. Instead they have fine hair-like growths called rhizoids that help them anchor onto bark, rocks, and soil. They act like sponges and absorb minerals from rain and moisture around them. Moss feels squishy and soggy to the touch and after the wet winter looked plump and vibrantly alive. During the drought years, the moss appeared so dried up to me that I doubted it would survive. But it turns out that moss is a hardy plant capable of living through extreme conditions from deserts to mountains. Moss does this by going dormant until conditions improve. Much as women's wisdom has gone dormant, hidden in fairy tales and proverbs, waiting for conditions to improve. On hot days, moss protects tree roots by insulating and shading the soil. These plants also provide shelter for insects to lay their eggs.

Sprinkled around the forest next to the moss are lichens. Lichens look like frilly, curled-up gray-green paper. Sometimes they appear powdery on the trunks of Douglas firs. They are made up of a species of algae combined with two different species of fungi. There are actually over three hundred species of fungi in the redwood forests.

We are beginning to learn about the foundational organisms in the soil, our own microbiomes, and species of plants like fungi. They create the environments that allow life to flourish. The beauty of life is apparent in the small details as well as the giant Roosevelt elk.

Joyful over my birthday hike, I skip up the trail, bursting into song and playing elf in the woods, talking to the trees. "You're beautiful," I throw my arms around a huge old redwood. "I love you."

My daughter laughs. "Do the trees talk back, Mom?"

"Of course," I answer, brushing my fingers over the rough serrated bark. It looks different on various redwoods: some spirals around, others are shaggy and ragged, and colors vary from pinky red to various shades of brown.

Michelle steps over a log, and I follow her up the trail. "What do the trees say?"

"They are happy growing."

"No." Michelle stops walking. "I mean what do they tell you? Are they excited about their next baseball game?"

I shake my head. "Trees don't play baseball. They aren't interested."

"So what do they talk about with each other?"

I shrug. "I'm not sure. The light they absorb from stars like our sun, the weather, nutrients in the soil, warning each other about dangerous insects, that sort of thing."

Michelle laughs. "My dog, Sooner, talks too. Sometimes Nate and I talk for him." She imitates her boyfriend pretending to be Sooner, "I like you best, Dad," and then pitches her voice high in her own silly imitation of her mini-poodle, "That's not true! Mom is my favorite."

I can't help thinking how interesting it is that Nate and Michelle have been rivaling each other over who their dog likes best. My daughters, born on the same day five years apart, ceaselessly try to get me to tell them which one is my favorite. I always reply that I love them both and don't have favorites. You'd think that by the ages of thirty and thirty-five they could give up the competition, but it seems there is no end in sight. Returning to my conversation with Michelle, I observe, "We might be getting a bit anthropomorphic."

"You think?" says Michelle, who is a civil engineer like her father, and both of them, living comfortably in the reality of the proven, think I'm nuts. A harmless, friendly sort of nuts but nuts nevertheless.

I *am* imaginative. Sometimes I'm not sure where the border between pure fantasy and reality actually is since some of my fantasies have come true. When I began spending time in the forest, I'd often pretend the forest was a wise sentient being with healing powers. Mushrooms, trees, birds, and butterflies watched me with friendly curiosity. Even the water knew my name.

I didn't expect anything to happen. By that time, I'd already resigned myself to living with chronic illness. Nothing had healed me until I began spending time with the trees. Some years later, the science about the benefits of forest bathing became public, and I realized what I thought was only an imaginary game had been proven. Fantasizing that I was being healed by a sentient forest worked. The combination of opening myself up to the imaginal realm and the forest environment simultaneously was more powerful than either one on its own.

There's a playful side of myself that feels free to come out in the woods. Sometimes I'm just plain silly. Often in my life I've noticed that silly behavior is equated with a lack of intelligence. We are conditioned to associate a serious demeanor with intelligence and are more likely to listen to people who talk in slow, low measured tones. Men speak in lower, usually slower tones and they've had dominant power for quite a long time now. In an attempt at adaptation for survival, women adopted fawning behaviors or imitated the style of men. Many of us cut our hair short, wore suits, and lowered our voices to be heard.

We've toned ourselves down, boxing ourselves in from the lighthearted, joyous expression that often matches our elemental natures. Creation is exuberant. We are in creation, creating. We are being created while we are creating. It's magnificent!

I don't want to have to act somber and solemn to be taken seriously. If that's my sole choice, I guess I'd rather not be listened to. It's more important to keep the spark of the holy fool alive within me, inspired and wise, laughing at myself and being able to see the humor in life.

I've heard that when the colonizers first came to Turtle Island (America), they saw the indigenous people dancing and singing and howling at the moon. Europeans immediately assumed from this joyful behavior that the native people were primitive, childlike, and lacking in intelligence. The only people in European society allowed to behave with such carefree abandonment were children under the age of seven.

I'm a one-woman rebellion, holding onto my silliness as if it were a raft of salvation in this dismembered culture. Even now, with all these very serious problems, can we kick up our heels and dance across the forest floor, letting in a little unicorn magic now and then? Sure, people may think we're not all that bright. I mean, the goofy lady talks to unicorns, right? Ergo, I don't have to take her seriously about anything. "I'll listen to people who don't waste their time skipping through the forest and cavorting with the chipmunks," says the serious adult. But what if the chipmunks are where it's at?

We can smile back and reply, "Let us know when you want to come out and play. We're here to greet the day. And oh, what a glorious day. The sun is shining. Flowers are blooming. Trees are growing. Songbirds chirp and cheep, twittering merrily. Isn't it amazing? To be alive in all this."

Forest Guidance

What makes you laugh? Laughter is good for us. According to the Mayo Clinic, it stimulates the organs, increases our intake of oxygen, releases feel-good endorphins, soothes tension, relieves pain, improves mood, and lowers blood pressure and heart rate. There is so much humor to be found in nature, from polka-dotted puffer fish to improbable animals like zebras and giraffes. Perhaps the big, fat frog leaping across the forest floor will make you laugh. If it does, you may find, as I so often have, that it is safe to let loose with gales of giggles and deep belly laughs in the spaciousness of a natural environment. One of the things I've loved most about being in wild places is that sometimes there is no one around for miles. No one is watching me, I can sing, dance, belly laugh, and express myself in ways that I'd be too inhibited to allow if I were around people, unless we were in some sort of freeing workshop. It often feels like the environment responds to my chortling; frogs croak, birds sing, plants wave their leaves in nonexistent breezes. Sometimes I think the whole world is just waiting for us to join in the fun—the sheer joy of existence.

27
Elen of the Ways

When we have the balance between the sacred masculine
and divine feminine, life flourishes.

After hearing about Elen of the Ways at Ancestor Tree, I sometimes make-believe that I am her, wandering in my forest, a
deer-antlered goddess. I see deer all the time in my backyard. They are
such feminine-looking animals, with big doe eyes and elegant, graceful
bodies with their fine, tapered legs. In the late spring, I look out the
window and watch bucks rub their newly grown antlers on tree trunks
to remove the itchy velvety coating. In fall, the bucks bash their antlers
together in fierce fights for dominance, vying for who will be able to
mate with the does. Once the bucks were going at it so hard that part
of an antler broke off. This wasn't as tragic as losing a horn would have
been because antlers are shed and regrown every year.

Antlers look heavy and uncomfortable to me. As I walk along,
another Ellen in another time, going along her leafy green ways,
I'm glad that I'm not actually wearing antlers. Even without the
antlers, learning more about Elen of the Ways has been helping
me to see with my heart and open to the magic of life in a spirit of
gratitude.

This goddess is known by other names including: Elen of the
Roads, Elen Belipotent, Saint Elen, Helen of Caernarfon, and Elen

of the Hosts. She was actually a woman in the fourth century and is written about in the famous *Mabinogion*, a book of Welsh stories from the thirteenth century. Some people believe the *Mabinogion* characters are Christianized variations on stories of older gods. Elen has been seen as an old Celtic goddess of sovereignty. In one tale, the Roman emperor Macsen Wledig (based on an actual emperor called Magnus Maximus) has a dream about Elen in which she appears as literally the woman of his dreams, and he falls in love with her.* When he tries to kiss her, Macsen awakens, and she is, of course, not there. He is left longing and obsessed with her, and his health and that of the land begin to fail. This is a frequent motif in fairy tales: the ailing king and ailing land that can only be saved by union with a woman (the divine feminine). The land is always seen as feminine, and the king is the one who brings fertility. I think it is relevant today. If we are going to restore ourselves and quit destroying the land, we will have to reunite with the feminine aspects of ourselves and each other and give them the honor and respect they deserve. The king gives and the land receives to create abundance. When we have the balance between the sacred masculine and divine feminine, life flourishes. In his dream, Macsen is seeking this wholeness.

Macsen sends thirteen messengers to find the woman he saw in his vision, telling them exactly where to go, based on his dream. They travel down a river and across a sea to the island of Britain and then to a castle at the mouth of a river, where Elen resides. The messengers tell Elen how the emperor is in love with her and ask her to return to Rome with them. Elen, a goddess of sovereignty, refuses and says that if he loves her, Macsen will travel to her. Macsen does exactly that, marching overland with his army to the island of Britain, where he defeats King Beli Mawr and conquers Britain, and

---

*See Evans, "British Legends"; and Shaw, "Elen of the Ways."

then travels on to the castle by the river. There he proposes to Elen, and she finally agrees to marry him.

As a goddess of sovereignty, Elen is powerful. She is also known as a warrior goddess who leads soldiers into battle. So one might say she is a protective goddess in her fierce ability to be a guardian of the land and all of its people. As a wedding gift, Elen asks for her father to be able to rule Britain, returning sovereignty to the conquered Britain. At her request, several castles are built, and she insists they be linked together by roads, hence her name Elen of the Ways.

Today as I walk on my forest path, I pass by a herd of deer in the large open meadow beside the redwood forest. A herd of elk grazes close by the deer, and I marvel at how they all seem to get along so well together, as I continue to ponder the myth of Elen of the Ways. It seems like such a compromise to me that she ends up marrying the man who conquers her lands, even if she does manage to negotiate so that her father continues to rule. This story operates within the context of dominance and invasion. Elen marries Macsen, and presumably that union with the divine feminine through her helps him and the land to heal. It must only be a partial healing, founded as it is on dominance, negotiation, and compromise.

To me, this does not feel like the full union of the divine feminine and the sacred masculine that will more deeply restore ourselves and the land. For that, Macsen would have had to find a peaceful way to come to Elen. Of course, warrior culture was thriving during the time this myth was written, and Rome was conquering much of the Western world, so it's easy to appreciate her sovereignty within the conditions of her times.

Centuries later we still experience warrior culture. I wonder if there is a way for us to live in another way and if a more harmonious balance between the sacred masculine and the divine feminine within and without would lead to it?

Forest Guidance

One place we can start to find the balance between the divine feminine and sacred masculine is to harmonize these qualities within ourselves. On the right side of the brain we have qualities traditionally defined as feminine (emotional, playful, creative, timeless flow, and euphoria) and on the left those that have been defined as masculine (organization, logic, planning for the future, and warning systems). All of us need both sets of qualities, no matter how we label them. Integrating these qualities in our personal and collective lives is the holy union within and without, the sacred marriage that can revitalize us and the land. A healthy environment, such as a forest, is a place of exquisite balance.

Go to the most intact wilderness you can find and notice the way nature brings together many elements to create a beautiful and functional ecosystem. As you sit, allow your mind to observe the various life-forms, paying attention to the relationships you see: tall trees shading a deep emerald pool and keeping it cool so fish thrive, an osprey diving for those fat fish and returning to a nest high in a redwood to feed the shrilly crying baby birds, and their bird droppings adding phosphorus and nitrogen to the soil, which helps the trees grow. Soaking in this exquisite balance, where no life-form or element of nature is left out or less valued, let yourself appreciate all the qualities of your being. To balance more deeply, try this exercise: Block the right nostril with your thumb, inhale through the left nostril. Use another finger to hold both nostrils closed. Hold for a few seconds and then exhale through the right nostril. Repeat on the other side. Continue until you feel relaxed, calm, and balanced.

28

The One-Hearted Path

*The path of humanity reconnecting in love with Earth
looks glossy, green, and beautiful.*

Elen of the Ways reminds me of Lady Galadriel, Queen of the Elves in Tolkien's trilogy. Both of them dwell in forests and have magical powers. The ancient redwood forest is so mystical, with an almost living light, a sort of diamond plasma, numinously shimmering in the trees. Plasma is produced when a neutral gas is heated up to the point where electrons are ripped away from atoms, forming an ionized gas. This gas has equal numbers of positively charged ions and negatively charged particles (electrons). It glows as nebulas, auroras, and stars. Plasma has been called the fourth state of matter, along with solids, liquids, and gases. But I've never heard of anyone seeing it glowing like a see-through jellyfish between the trees in the woods. Still, the words *crystal* or *diamond plasma* are the ones that come into my mind when I try to describe this barely perceivable substance that feels like some sort of creative substrate of life.

Looking around at the living green, I'm aware that a magical part of myself comes alive in the forest. I can almost remember how to direct this intelligent plasma in ways that generate more beauty, healing, and joy. There's a deep part of me that seems to know: Elen of the Ways, Lady Galadriel, and the Golden Lady with the Lion who has inhabited my imaginal realm since I was a teenager all merge into one powerful interior goddess of my becoming.

I am the goddess walking as I stride confidently up the trail. To one side, a large stream splashes cheerfully. Glimpsing small emerald pools with sand and gravel banks, I round a bend and continue to hike through enormous trees. Trees that spire over me so that I feel as small as an ant. Trees that seem to exude this plasma the same way they breathe out oxygen. There are still a few mushrooms along the trail. Coral fungus has sprouted up again after the recent rain. About six inches tall with wavy tendrils, I marvel at how a pinkish-orange one does look like undersea coral. I've seen yellow, white, and red ones too.

Today, I'm going to sit with one of the largest redwood trees I visit. She hasn't revealed a name to me yet, so I simply call her Grandmother as I take my seat at her base. As soon as I close my eyes, breathing in, pausing, breathing out, pausing, the diamond plasma light envelops me. I'm in a womb of impalpable substance made out of light. The thick light feels so knowing. It permeates my pores, awakens my cells, and infuses me with my own sort of gnosis.

A pileated woodpecker with a characteristic tuft of red on its head tap-tap-taps near me on a hollow tree trunk. Probably foraging for ants. I hope the bird leaves enough ants to plant the trillium seeds, I think, listening to the taps get louder so that now they sound like a drum. I know these woodpeckers tend to nest in snags and dead trees, and there is a large stump nearby with a big cavity. Redwoods often have cave-like openings in their trunks, called basal hollows. They are created when fires reach the heartwood. Later fires cause the center of the tree to decay, and this forms tree caves. It's very hard to meditate with the bird drumming away right next to my head, but I still try.

Then it starts shrieking, a sound like hysterical laughter, *cuk-cuk-cuk* rising and falling in pitch. I give up. Opening my eyes, I glimpse light trails flickering around the tree. Angelic elementals? At my feet, elementals sprout up from the ground, unfolding their see-through bodies like plants. "Love Earth. That's all you need to do," they chorus sweetly. Water elementals shimmer agreement from the dewdrops cupped in a nearby frond.

"I do love Earth," I say aloud.

"Birds, animals, crystals, rivers, and waters are all a part of you." The information floats into my head. Is this from the tree?

Maybe the tree is speaking for herself. Animals shelter in her boughs, birds have nests high in her canopy, and clearly some are even boring holes in neighboring trunks. The tree drinks the water, and her essence feels so pure it is crystalline. I know this tree is teaching and guiding me.

The woodpecker finally takes a break, and I sit with the tree in the hushed quiet of the forest. I'm very relaxed when another thought floats in, "To find your way, ask, What is the next step love would take?"

Certainly sitting here.

"We all came here to bless the world," adds the old wise tree. "Bless the world with our presences, our beings, and the gifts of our nature."

Suddenly, I see myself as a giant sunflower, offering seeds. What will these seeds become? Who will they nourish? Will they grow more sunflowers?

Nature embraces all duality and doesn't place a higher value on night or day, life or death, old or young. It is all part of the organic process of arising and disintegrating. All part of the completeness of being.

Grounding into my earth star chakra six inches below my seat, the energy travels up through my first through seventh chakras, and I feel heat quickening each area. Above my head, I connect with my soul star chakra and then the spirit, universal, and divine gateway chakras. I can feel the tree equally streaming light in this vertical alignment, heaven and Earth, one ecosystem of moon, stars, sun, and Gaia.

Future probabilities unfold in my mind's eye. In one, humans have fouled the water and air to the point where we make our bodies increasingly artificial to survive, so that we become some sort of hybrid artificial intelligence. It feels like one of those old science-fiction horror stories I read as a kid.

In another one, we have all sorts of machines and high-tech inventions, sucking carbon out of the air and even dimming the sun. The birds hate this. Another science-fiction horror movie.

Another one shows me children with wires growing out of their heads. They are so attached to screens that distinguishing between virtual and real reality is almost a lost art.

In some visions, there are no human beings or many other species left on Earth.

The path of humanity reconnecting in love with Earth looks glossy, green, and beautiful. We learn to mimic nature and allow her to guide us as we find balanced ways to live without destroying the life around us. We fall in love with her beauty and sometimes enhance it in gardens and sacred groves.

This path the tree shows me is one small ribbon around a Maypole of ribbons, one thread in a tapestry. It looks thin and insubstantial, but it is as available as any of the other paths. We can choose it.

A sigh ripples from the tree through me. It's as if the tree knows her metaphorical vision has been successfully conveyed, and I know that I am supposed to share the tree's vision.

I wouldn't take this too seriously; I *am* imaginative after all. But I remember a vision I had repeatedly while sitting with the trees over a decade ago. I never had it anywhere else, but when I was in the presence of the ancient trees, I kept seeing living green corridors connecting forests and other wild places with one another. When I shared that vision with a young woman who had graduated from Harvard in environmental engineering, she was so inspired that she applied for and received grants to create these corridors between wild places!

A squirrel scatters some debris, and a redwood cone lands on my head, a sort of confirmation. Getting up and brushing needles off my

clothes, I hike back down the trail, thinking about the many prophecies about the times we are living in. As noted earlier, Hopi prophecies
suggest that our fourth world will end from changes in the weather,
loss of wildlife, floods, famines, social disruptions, and wars. Sadly, it
looks like we are right on schedule. But it's not hopeless. Like similar prophecies, the Hopi suggest from petroglyphs found on their
Prophecy Rock that we do have a choice; it is possible to return to the
one-hearted path of living closer to nature, grounded in the rhythms
of Earth and in accordance with the will of the Creator.

Forest Guidance

I'm vowing right now to choose the one-hearted path in every way I possibly can in my daily life. This means that I refuse to allow any part of me to dominate; my intellect doesn't override my heart, my mind doesn't force my body, and I try to quiet myself enough to listen to my soul. In order to do this, I have to slow down—something that I find much easier to do in a wild ecosystem. When I do this, sometimes I perceive the diamond plasma, which seems alive and aware of us. Playing with this intelligent substance in the space between trees and other natural forms, I sense that the plasma is also playing with me, as eager and responsive as a puppy. If you'd like to join me in playing with the diamond plasma, go to a wild place. Imagine the space between objects is intelligent and alive; the birth place of All-That-Is. Pretend you can shape it with your hands, speak it into physical matter with words, and sing it into various expressions of life. Imagine your thoughts, visions, ideas, heart wishes, prayers, and blessings all influencing this responsive light. What if we could co-create with this barely perceptible energy?

29
Violet Tree

Nature intelligence is so eager to work
with us in restoring our world.

When I return home and tell Allegra how I saw the diamond plasma again, she replies, "I think that light is eager to play with us."

"You're right. I need to go back to the trees. It's powerful right now. Do you want to go with me tomorrow?" I ask.

"Yes. I think so. Let's decide in the morning."

"Sure," I reply. That's how we always do it. We are "following the juice," a technique a lama in the Tibetan Buddhist tradition taught us. Following the juice involves being guided by our heart wishes and what gives us more life-force energy. It helps to have some unscheduled time in our lives so that we can feel into what we, especially our bodies, want to do next. We choose the next most loving thing to do moment to moment. Cluttering up the calendar removes many chances to have this freedom. Most likely, the two of us will awaken eager to go to the forest. But if either or both of us does not, it's no big deal. I'm happy to go alone. And maybe I won't feel like going at all. But I think I will. I usually do. "What tree do you want to visit?" I ask.

"I wish we could go to Summer Tree," Allegra answers a bit wistfully.

I'm yearning for Summer Tree too. We often practiced restorative yoga on the flat soft forest floor in front of her. "The river is still way too high to cross."

"I know," agrees Allegra. "How about Spiral Tree?" Spiral Tree has bark that swirls around the trunk in ascending spirals. We love that tree because the trail is relatively untraveled and we rarely see anyone else.

"The trail is a mess from downed trees. Steve and I had to crawl."

"It's too bad we can't go to Winter Tree anymore," says Allegra.

"Yeah." We both know that's out of the question. Since COVID lockdown had more people getting outside, and all the information came out about the benefits of forest bathing, the parks have been much more crowded. There are way too many people on that trail to have a deep meditation at Winter Tree the way we used to do.

"We could go to Violet Tree. We haven't been there in a long time."

"Good idea," I agree, and we leave it there knowing that we will be pulled somewhere on the morrow. The trees seem to call us. Actually, I think the trees and wild nature in general are calling all of us. Nature intelligence is so eager to work with us in restoring our world. The nature spirits and elementals love Earth and want to heal what has been harmed.

The next day, we are both eager to go. On the forty-minute drive to the state park, Allegra and I pass ocean waves crashing against cliffs. Forests line slopes almost down to the sea. In the distance, we glimpse snow-covered hills, which we know roll up to mountains. Catching ourselves up on the details of our lives, we chatter. Steve can never figure out how we understand each other, the way we talk, finishing each other's sentences, leaving some things half said, interjecting, adding, digressing, and embellishing. But we do understand. We both feel heard and listened to as we share. I mention my granddaughter has a fever and has been throwing up, so I'm feeling worried about her and my daughter, who is stressed juggling being a mother and a teacher. Allegra tells me about her partner's coming knee surgery and how she is driving out of the area for the procedure, which is expensive since she will have to stay in a hotel while he's in the hospital. We also share our grief at seeing so many trees down and that climate change is raging. As we listen to each other, the worry and stress lighten.

Parking the car, we shoulder our daypacks stuffed with lunch, first-aid kits, rain gear, and canteens with water. Once we enter the forest, we begin our silence. This allows us to become more fully present. We notice what we see (green, green, green), hear (birds, trickling water, the soughing of branches in the breeze), smell (moist, loamy soil), taste (redwood sorrel, miner's lettuce, a sip of water), touch (the fresh air on our faces), and sense (the intelligent energy in the space between trees).

Exposed roots crisscrossing the steep trail are slick from recent rain, and Allegra and I are glad we have our poles. I am extra careful as I walk because the tiny crystals that all of us have in our inner ears went out of place, and for the past week I have felt a little dizzy. Walking in silence, we go into a sort of rhythmic trance. Tendrils of fog wrap around branches.

A large northern red-legged frog hops in front of us. We stop and stare. The frog is pretty big, about three inches long. Noticing the black spots on the frog's reddish-brown skin, I say, "I wonder how old this frog is?"

"Let's ask the frog," replies Allegra. "How old are you, Froggie?"

We look more closely. The frog has something furry in its mouth. A caterpillar? They do eat caterpillars and beetles, I think, watching it swallow. "I read people hunted these frogs to eat their legs to the point they were threatened."

Allegra wrinkles her nose. "Slimy."

"Yeah. Now I think their biggest threat is habitat destruction. They need wetlands to live."

The frog blinks, lids flicking closed for an instant over big, bulging yellow eyes with a vertical black pupil. Then the frog boings off into the five-fingered ferns on the side of the path.

Allegra and I laugh. There's something hilarious about these big, ungainly frogs. It's great to see a robust frog as amphibians are sensitive to environmental changes and act as indicator species that show the health of an ecosystem.

Resuming our companionable silence, Allegra and I hike up the trail. It's a good workout. My heart is pounding, and I am enjoying the feeling of breathing in so deeply, fresh oxygenated air clearing my lungs.

An hour later, we make our way to Violet Tree. She's not the biggest or most impressive tree in the forest, but she stands a bit off the trail with other trees along a ridge. It's a lovely, sheltered place to be, with warm sunbeams sparkling between the trees. Settling down beside her, I cross my legs in a half lotus and sit with my back close to, but not touching, the trunk. Lichen grows up the trunk in shades of green and yellow, and I don't want to rub it off. Allegra parks herself nearby at a similar tree. In fact, I'm not sure which tree we've actually named Violet Tree; the violet rays seem to come through both trees. We chant Tara mantras for a while, which helps us feel more centered and calm, ready to tune into the trees.

Today is an easy day to meditate. They aren't all the same. Some days I am restless; some days the trees feel less available. But sometimes the energy between Gaia and the cosmos seems lined up and conducive. Today is one of those days, and I feel an immediate sense of tingling up and down my spine.

The small quartz rock at my feet glows, like solidified light. Picking it up, I feel a tiny light being living inside the crystal. Holding the stone close to my heart, a wave of gentle healing emanates out of the crystal and my heart opens so that I'm better able to sense the tree at my back.

Suddenly I'm envisioning myself in a past life as a young woman in China. My feet are bound so that I can hardly walk. I teeter along to my seat where I work long hours sorting through vats of silk worms. The worms eat mulberry leaves and then spin cocoons of silk filaments. Later, like a butterfly, the cocooned worm metamorphoses into a silk moth. Instead of allowing the moths to live, my job is to throw the cocoons into boiling water. I'm boiling the worms alive. Thousands and thousands of worms. It makes me sick. My religion tells me not to kill. Why don't worms count? I would leave if I could, but I have no choice about doing this work. I'm a slave, although no one calls me one. Men are attracted to my tiny feet and think they are beautiful. I hate them. I want to walk. I want to dance and run free. I vow that I will never have another life with tiny feet.

And here I am. I must be satisfying the vow now, spending so much of my life tramping around the forest with my big feet in my even bigger boots.

Releasing the vision, I continue to breathe until I enjoy a moment of pure peace. Behind my closed eyes, I notice shimmering violet colors forming into geometric configurations. Light enters my crown, filling my heart. Why does it look violet to my inner eyes when I'm with this tree?

Noticing the crystal still held in my palm, I feel the little fairy inside. She wants me to regain a lost spiritual gift from my life as a Chinese woman in a silk factory. Is it the gift of empathy? To feel the pain of those small worms, boiled alive?

I know that even at the height of my arachnophobia, looking into a spider's eyes has always given me chills. Clearly they are intelligent and conscious beings. As are bees and hummingbirds and every single living creature.

Inhaling. Exhaling. Warmth in my belly. Violet light courses through my nervous system, cleansing, clearing, and healing. About twenty years ago, I had a hands-on healer clear my field using Saint Germain and the violet flame. Saint Germain is purported to be a man who was a master of ancient spiritual teachings. He was a count who was also an alchemist and musician. Whether or not he was a real spiritual master, the violet flame technique worked, and I left the healer feeling better. Now a similar violet flame is coming to me spontaneously at the trees.

New Age lore says that the Age of Aquarius will be infused with the seventh, violet ray. This ray is a powerful source of self-transformation. It can heal physical health problems, negative emotions, and even karma. Violet is the color for the crown chakra. This is the chakra that connects us to more cosmic consciousness, healing abilities, agape (selfless love), and enhances creative ability.

Right now, the violet ray runs through my body and I feel it clearing stuck places. The flame blazes through the right side of my head, and I feel choked up. Tears run down my face, and my Eustachian tube between my ear and my nose prickles, like little acupuncture needles have been placed there. My ear feels hot to the touch. Giving a short, sharp shake to my head, which I instinctively know is exactly the right movement, my long, slightly frizzy hair swirls around my face. I've kept it long ever since I had a bad haircut in fifth grade that made me feel shorn like a sheep, bald and bare, my ears flaming with shame. In fifth grade I wanted to look like a princess. Smoothing my out-of-control, unruly hair down, it occurs to me that it was the embarrassment from that haircut that the violet light cleared.

The slightly dizzy feeling I've been having is gone. What a relief. Did the violet flame help my ear crystals settle back into place?

Closing my eyes again, I go into a simple breathing meditation and feel that relaxing sense of my head expanding and letting go so that I have a little more room to be. Violet light continues to dazzle behind my closed eyelids, and I watch it, mesmerized, awed at the way my body, with the help of the energy channeled down from the tree, actually knew how to heal. I'd tried everything, including the Epley maneuver, to get those ear crystals back into place.

But clearly it wasn't solely the crystals that were the problem; it was the old, stuck energy of shame. To feel better, I had to solve the problem both physically, emotionally, spiritually, and mentally. And to do that, I had to have enough free time to sit still in the forest and allow myself to be healed.

Forest Guidance

Being able to practice forest bathing or any sort of nature therapy requires setting aside a certain amount of time for that purpose. One way is to put visiting your favorite locations on the calendar as a scheduled event. If you have the time to leave some open-ended space in your life, that's even better. It's so lovely to wake up and figure out what we want to do that day. That leaves us available to intuit where we are drawn. I've found that certain spots call me at different times. When I need a feeling of spaciousness, the beach is great. For perspective and clarity, I love to climb a mountain. To relax, laugh, and feel into my playful, feminine otter side, there is nothing like a creek or a river. The forest is fabulous for healing and introspection. And, of course, these environments might stimulate you in different ways than they do for me. Giving ourselves a little space allows us more room to listen in and discover what our heart and soul desires.

30
Freyja

We can grow gratitude like a weed, precious and profuse.

Part of coming into my wholeness includes accepting the part of myself that is assertive and can say no, like the warrior goddesses. In this book, I left out the part about Freyja being a warrior goddess. I don't like fighting. I don't like war. I want nothing to do with it. But the Norse goddess Freyja, along with many of the Celtic goddesses in my personal ancestry, such as the Morrigan, Maeve, and Boudica, are warriors. Stories have it that some of the women in Ireland didn't sit back and let the invading Romans take over; instead, they grabbed swords or whatever they had handy and went howling and shrieking into battle. These embodied goddesses were defending their homes, children, and land to the death. They'd rather die than be raped.

During the five hundred years of English colonization in Ireland, the fierce women and men did not win in their attempts to save their land and culture. Their sacred trees were cut down to build boats and for charcoal. Worst of all, the colonizers forbade the Irish to own trees or even seeds. As with the takeover of many indigenous cultures, sub-jugating the people involved taking over their land and severing their deep relationships with nature. It makes sense that healing ourselves will likewise involve a return to our intimate relationship with Earth.

We have models for how the warrior goddesses within us might react to violating situations. When Freyja, a shield maiden known as a Valkyrie, wearing a falcon feather dress that allows her to shape-shift into a raptor, attracts the unwelcome sexual attention of a giant, she doesn't hesitate to fight back. The giant makes a bargain with the gods, including the thunder god Thor, to build a wall around their home if they will give him Freyja as his wife. She knows nothing about this agreement, and when the time comes for the gods to make good on their part of the deal by giving Freyja in marriage, she will not cooperate to the point where Thor is forced to dress up as Freyja to fake the marriage contract!*

What Freyja does not do is quietly accept a circumstance that violates her sovereignty. Neither should we for ourselves or the land. As we restore the land, all of us will have the chance to deepen our relationships with nature, as both individuals and communities.

Part of this restoration is to heal ourselves because it is our severed selves that have allowed this paradigm of subjugating nature to spread like a virus. Many of us have learned to subjugate our own bodies with a mind-over-matter attitude. Forcing our bodies to go, go, go when they are begging for rest, some of us collapse with autoimmune diseases or chronic fatigue, as I did. Sometimes this unsustainable lifestyle is so deeply embedded into the culture that we don't have much choice if we and our families are going to survive. That was certainly my case when my daughters were little. We didn't have local family to help or the financial resources to hire people, so both Steve and I had to work harder than was comfortable. But sometimes the circumstances change, and there is more room to slow down, only we've forgotten how, including on vacations or after retirement. Even in the busiest life, there is often a little wriggle room to choose some quiet time, going to bed an hour earlier, taking a nap, skipping

---

*See Asgard, "The Tale of Thor's Wedding."

events that we think we "should" go to when we yearn for a cozy moment curled up with a good book or spending quiet time in our favorite outdoor spot.

Another way we mercilessly push our bodies is by not setting boundaries and saying no. People pleasers like I was are prone to this—tending to be more tuned into what other people want from us than what we ourselves want. Often, when we don't say no, our bodies will say it for us by getting sick or having accidents.

We swallow our grief and hide our sorrows in addictions to food, drugs, sex, shopping, alcohol, or scrolling mindlessly through social media. It's worth taking a moment to consider where we are denying and overriding ourselves, repressing our heart's desires, and not taking the time to listen to what our deepest wishes are.

How we treat our bodies is similar to how we treat nature. According to 8 Billion Trees, a carbon-offset company that runs large-scale tree planting operations, a staggering fifteen billion trees are cut down every year. We whip the land into overproduction with artificial fertilizers, never allowing the soil to rest. We move Earth's flows with dams and canals. We pave over, pound down, and pare away the places where nature tries to burst forth in her glorious living green. We don't ask and seek permission from Gaia when we want to make changes to her body. We violate ourselves, each other, and Mother Earth.

It doesn't have to be violence, domination, taking without asking, and power over others. We can change. We can gently tend Earth and each other, making love with All-That-Is in a co-creative relationship. We already see this beginning to happen with courses on nonviolent communication, ideas that sex must at the very least be consensual, forest gardens, permaculture, biodynamic gardening, and restoring woodlands and wetlands.

Notice Earth. She is not always passive and giving, although certainly all of our abundance comes from Earth. She can rebalance with terrifying earthquakes, volcanos, hurricanes, floods, and fires.

When the time is right, we can roar.

And we can also forgive ourselves and one another. It's one thing to stand up and roar and say, "Stop! I do not consent to this." It is another thing to hold the anger inside and let it fester. Then the poison is in us, and we are the ones harmed. Forgiving does not mean dropping the discernment that allows us to know when we need to protect ourselves, choosing what is healthy to allow into our lives. It does mean understanding that the sacred masculine is as wounded and damaged as the divine feminine.

We cultivate what promotes peace and health. This is both personal and universal. We can take care of our precious bodies, the part of Earth that allows us to be here and partake of this experience of life. We can also tend the environment, cultivating healthy soil, clean water, and clean air, as well as planting plants where they can thrive. As we cultivate well-being in our landscapes, we also must befriend our inner ecology. We can grow gratitude like a weed, precious and profuse. When we start looking, it is not hard for most of us to find things to be grateful for. Our lives, for a start.

And the life all around us. A squirrel fluffs a bushy gray tail as he climbs Star Tree. Star flowers bloom delicate pink at my feet. Cirrus clouds cross the sky, changing shapes, so I can see dragons winking at me from above. Cushioned in thick needles, I lie back close to the solid trunk of the tree, overwhelming gratitude filling my heart. Gaia is lavish with her ever-changing and rearranging beauty. Somehow in this state of fulfilling peace, it seems possible that we can protect love and innocence. We can sprinkle kindness at every opportunity. We can defend the space within and without ourselves in our shared world with all of the fierceness of our love. Rise up warrior goddesses, the time is now.

Forest Guidance

Saying no can give us more spaciousness in our lives to say yes to what we do want. No is a protective boundary that allows the tender parts of ourselves to bloom. Often when we agree to do something that we don't want to do, it is so that people will like and approve of us. Paradoxically, when what we do is not right for us, it doesn't usually end up being right for other people either, and we do not receive the yearned-for approval. Since our time and energy are not limitless, it is important to choose what we wish to cultivate. Going alone into the wilderness helps us to touch more deeply into ourselves and find the inner guidance that points the way. Sit with nature and feel into what you want to say no to. Where is your yes? What do you want to put your energy into? Make some room for that. It could be spending more time in nature, as it was for me.

31
Missed Chances

*Sometimes last chances sneak up on us before
we know they are last chances.*

Part of rising up is taking care of ourselves, so I'm practicing yoga in my sunroom, gazing out the window at Grandmother Dragon Tree. I hear her faint whisper in my mind, "Don't miss your chances."

Staring at my poor bedraggled apple tree, I think about the chance I missed to paint the tree when she was in full white-blossomed glory, symmetrical and gorgeous. Next year, I thought, as spring turned to summer and blossoms became fruit. Abundant apples hung like ornaments from all her branches. Attracted by the delicious fruit, a bear came and climbed the tree, breaking off two of her large limbs. I woke up to a diminished tree. She still valiantly blossoms and fruits, but that moment of perfection has never come again and now exists in my mind as a fading memory.

Watching ravens circle and then perch on Grandmother Dragon Tree's high branches, I think-ask back, "Did you mean my chance to paint the apple tree in bloom?"

I don't receive an answer. Instead, into my reclining shavasana pose floats the memory of COVID and how I missed some chances. Before COVID, there were places I planned to go and people I planned to visit. I'd been putting the trips off, waiting for more time, money, and energy.

Kraa, kraa, kraa interject the ravens circling the tree, as if confirming that I'm on the right thought track. Their voices sound deeper and raspier than crows, and they are bigger too. Continuing to let myself go limp and almost boneless, inhaling deeply, exhaling fully, I think about how so much changed when COVID struck. We were locked down. Steve was high risk. My doctor told me I was too, due to age. I felt well and might have ignored her advice, but I had to protect Steve. So I stayed home. I figured once COVID was over, I would prioritize travel to visit those friends and family. I wouldn't put it off again.

The official pandemic lasted over three years. By the time it ended, some of those opportunities to visit people and go places had vanished. People had moved, become ill, or even died.

The ravens fly off. Grandmother Dragon Tree sighs in my mind. I sigh too, letting out a long sad breath.

Opportunities do not last forever. Sometimes we can miss our chances. Our homes are literally blowing away, burning down, and brimming with floodwaters before we are collectively even admitting climate change is real and *talking* about doing something. Humanity has proven with COVID that we can act fast when we believe we are threatened; in a matter of weeks, much of the world was locked down. Our carbon emissions significantly dropped as people worked more from home and didn't fly as much. It was stressful to change our lifestyles practically overnight, but it was also stunning to witness the speed with which we could do so.

We seem to have fallen into the same delusion with the climate crisis that I did with my own travel plans, thinking I had plenty of time. Bypassing chance after chance to slow global warming down makes it appear we think there will be many future chances. But what if there aren't? Scientists, mystics, and indigenous prophecies all indicate that the time is now; they say we have five or ten years left to determine whether or not we leave a habitable world for our great-grandchildren and many other species. It's all happening so fast, with exponentially escalating effects as various systems destabilize.

I recall my recent visit with Stevie, my three-year-old granddaughter, and how fascinated she was on our neighborhood walk with snails, ants, butterflies, and birds. I so want her to inherit a world of life. She said, "Birds are my favorite." Later she said, "Butterflies are my favorite." After that, "Flowers are my favorite." Smiling to myself, I think Stevie has it right. What a lovely way to live life, going from one favorite to the next on this bountiful planet.

Then my heart clenches. It's too painful to even think about these favorites not always being here for her. Sometimes last chances sneak up on us before we know they are last chances. We don't know if this is our absolute last chance to turn the climate crisis around and head the other direction, but maybe we should behave as if it is.

Sitting up, I comfort myself with the flowers in vases all around my house: bright yellow daffodils, calla lilies, purple and yellow iris, sweet columbines, rhododendrons, and glorious big peonies. Steve has planted so many flowers around the house that I live in a flower bower. Flowers give me hope. Fragile and delicate, almost improbable in their varied and astonishing loveliness, and yet here, year after year. "I love you," I say to the daffodils. And they beam their bright beauty back to me.

Forest Guidance

Trying to accomplish things all at once, in a big leap, is a recipe for overwhelm and burnout. Instead, think of one opportunity you have right now, today, and take it. Perhaps it is to cheer yourself up by arranging flowers in a vase, giving someone a hug, watering a thirsty plant, communing with trees, or standing up to protect a freshwater source. Whatever it is, our dreams are accomplished one small action at a time. The Japanese have a word, *kaizen*, which means "change for the better" or "continuous improvement." I know that I've climbed mountains that looked too hard to ascend, but I got to the top by taking one little step after another. What opportunity can you take today that you don't want to miss?

32
Camping

Choosing realities is big magic.

One thing I know I don't want to miss is the opportunity to go camping, so Steve and I are off to the redwoods. We love falling asleep in the tent, listening to the *shhh* of the river and the occasional *whoo-who-whoo-who* of an owl. We are nestled into the embrace of the forest all around us. At night, the trees' whispers grow louder, fronds rustling overhead, lulling me into sleep. I dream with the redwoods.

My dreams are peace. They are stillness, like the trees standing tall and aware of the moon behind the night fog. My dreams are laced with the honey of being with a forest of tree friends. It is so safe here, so undisturbed, that I let go completely and plummet into a somnolence so profound that I don't remember my dreams.

Instead, I awaken nine hours later completely refreshed, restored in a way I have not felt in a long time. Lying beneath my cozy, warm sleeping bag, I listen to birds greet the day, trying to recognize them by their songs. The single note of the varied thrush is easy to identify. Another bird sending off a series of high-pitched trills could be a Pacific wren. Sounding almost like an owl, there's the soft crooning coo of a California native pigeon. Maybe that's a western tanager singing with high and low notes, as if it is asking a question. I often see their bright yellow bodies flitting through the forest. So many more birds I don't know join the morning chorus: *tup-tup-tup, zee-zee-zee-bzz-bzz, wha-wha-wha, cheep-cheep-cheep.* The birds chirp their morning joy.

Listening to birdsongs increases mental well-being and lowers anxiety, depression, and even paranoia. The theory is that the sounds of nature lead us into a state of "soft fascination," where something holds our attention but does not take all of it. Wherever we are, we can enjoy these benefits because even listening to a recording of bird-song offers beneficial effects that can last for hours.*

Stretching luxuriously, I think about getting up and making a cup of hot tea for a long while before I actually put on my warm jacket and brave the chilly morning. Everything I do is slow, relaxed, and easy. There's no hurry, nowhere I have to go, because I'm already here and there's nowhere else I'd rather be. Steve is still snoring happily.

Once he gets up and drinks his morning coffee, I ask, "Where do you want to hike today?"

We talk about the various trails and trees, the possibilities for a day that already feels exquisite. "It will be warmer a bit inland," I say.

"Supposed to be in the eighties," agrees Steve.

"How about our river trail?" I suggest. I haven't been there in ages. Not since the day Allegra and I nearly stepped on a rattlesnake.

"We will have to watch out for rattlesnakes," Steve says, as if reading my mind.

"And ticks, poison oak, and cliffs," I joke, except I'm not really kidding.

"Sure," says Steve. "Let's do it."

We eat our nine-grain pancakes, pack lunches, and get in his truck to drive up the south fork of the river. We turn off onto a fairly long dirt road and come to the end. The parking area is empty. It is remote out here.

Glad I have my poles to thump the ground since snakes do not

---

*Sima, "Why Birds and Their Songs Are Good for Our Mental Health."

hear but instead feel vibrations, we head off down the trail, feeling ebullient. The sky is cerulean blue. The day already feels warm.

Inland a bit from the redwood forests, we are in a slightly hotter, drier climate with huge old madrones with their satiny red bark and lots of Douglas firs. The trail is narrow, with cliffs on my left side. Below the river winds through the canyon like a green silk ribbon interspersed with lacey whitewater.

We stop a couple miles in at a fern grotto with water tumbling over the mossy green stepping-stones. It's such a fairy place that I think anyone can feel the fairies here. "Do you hear the fairies laughing?" I ask Steve.

"It's pretty here," he replies, stooping to fill our canteens. We treat the water with a UV filter and then drink this champagne of waters.

"Mmmm," I murmur. My body shivers with pure vibrancy. I'm reluctant to leave, but the emerald pools in the river beckon.

We hike high on a cliff, admiring the views up the canyon to snow-covered mountains. Rounding a bend, we come to the place where Allegra and I saw the snake. I point to the now swept-clean trail. The U.S. Forest Service or Civilian Conservation Corps must have cleared the rocks. Probably a good idea, since Allegra and I were pretty sure there was a whole nest of snakes. "That's where the piles of rocks used to be," I tell Steve. "I stepped right on top of a boulder and woke up the rattlesnake underneath. The snake snapped into a coil with the tip of her tail up in the ready-to-rattle position and poked her head out at Allegra."

Steve shakes his head. "Close one."

"The worst was that Allegra and I were on opposite sides of the rock with a rattler between us and cliffs on both sides." I point to the upside of the cliffs. "I had to crawl around that."

"No way," says Steve, and I see that for the first time he actually understands my story and how imperiled I was. "It looks impossible." Above where the nest of snakes used to be is a slide-shale cliff. Below is a steep ravine covered in poison oak. "How did you do it?"

"We were lucky," I say, now realizing exactly how lucky. "The snake was so wound up, we decided to meditate first, so I sat around the bend for twenty minutes. When I came back, Allegra said the snake was still coiled but no longer ready to rattle. I couldn't see it from my side. It was way too big of a leap for me to try jumping across the rock pile. There was no way back besides climbing around on that cliff."

"Crazy," says Steve.

"Yeah. First I threw my poles across and then my daypack. It was such a fortunate throw. The pack landed right between the snake and where I was about to slide down the other side of the cliff. At least the pack would be the one bitten and not me." I show Steve the slide. "Allegra stood there and helped me slow my speed when I came tumbling down."

"You could have kept falling all the way down the cliff!" exclaims Steve.

"And that was before I had a Garmin Mini," I reply. Garmin has put out an emergency satellite SOS for extremely expensive helicopter rescues.

"Bad place to be stuck." I can see from the way Steve shakes his head and his blue eyes widen that showing him the actual spot versus telling the story has made it real for him in a whole different way. This applies to our connections with nature. Talking and reading about nature or watching nature shows on TV is better than nothing, but the direct contact of touching a houseplant or opening a window to feel the air brings us in more deeply.

Wiping a cobweb off my face, I realize no one has traveled this trail in a long time. We continue hiking, and I feel a little sobered. At the time we awakened the snake, I did what I had to, one step at a time, and everything worked out. Looking back, I questioned if it was as scary as I remembered. Now that I'm here, I see it was much scarier.

One single slip, one wrong move with the snake, and I might not be here to write the story.

Today is beautiful, and everything goes smoothly. At long last, years later I make it down to the enticing emerald pools. The water is freezing and so rapid that I can only get in at a shallow side pool. Standing up to my waist, my skin is instantly numb and red.

Steve reclines in the shade on a "lounge chair" made of smooth basalt rock and stares at the rushing water. It is such a pleasure to see so much water everywhere after the years of drought. I sit next to him for a while but then am called to a quiet little mossy place beside a rivulet under the shade of an alder tree to meditate.

Sweet. Peaceful. Breathing in and out. How good it is to be in a wild place. My whole field is laundered and clear. It's paradoxical that the cleanest I ever feel is out camping on the ground, dirt under my fingernails. But the air is fresh and sweet, the water varying shades of blue, the trees vibrant with new leaf green. I revel in the pure undisturbed spaciousness of it all and am in heaven.

Letting the dulcet tones of the small rivulet lull me, I drift into a vision. I see moments in time arising in various artistic compositions, the elements of who, what, and where coming together in living streams of light.

The Blue Fairy Lady materializes before me. She's large—maybe three or four feet. Glittery. Shimmering. I've seen her ever since I was around eight years old alone in a mountain meadow in the Sierra Nevada Mountains. The silence and peace, the magnificence and beauty swept me in, and I had a moment of becoming raptor and bumblebee, butterfly and buttercup. I became the flower-filled meadow and the vast bowl of cobalt sky. I became the white granite mountains. And I was gifted with the Blue Fairy Lady.

Sometimes I think of her as Gaia's emissary, the voice and spirit of the land.

"Hello," I greet her.

The Blue Fairy Lady rarely speaks to me in words. She glistens and glows. She beckons and beams. She waves her wand, and the lid pops off the top of my head and I flutter in the sun-dappled leaves with her, skimming the surface of the silky river, touching lightly the sunbaked, serpentine green stones. We waltz around the canyon, flying in delight, showering fairy dust, as the Blue Fairy Lady leads me up into what appear to be temples made out of beams of light. Ethereal and airy, yet definitely there . . . maps of sound, light, sacred geometry, and color weave and morph before my eyes. They are imprints on the ether that simply exist: no past or future. It's all eternally happening now. What once was, is. What will be, is. What is now, is.

The Blue Fairy Lady with her dazzling dress, points her smooth manzanita wand at one hologram after another. As she does, they seem to grow more solid and substantial.

"We collectively pick which stories we wish to live," says the Blue Fairy Lady, tossing her head of glossy black curls. Her voice is rare and exquisite, like water burbling over pebbles, or the tinkling of leaves in a soft breeze, but I understand her perfectly. "Where we focus our attention actualizes potential realities," she continues, speaking more words to me at once than she ever has in my whole life. She points at one hologram after another. They flash with images of fighting, images of lovemaking, images of people feasting on greens and berries around an oval table. "Choosing realities is big magic." Her wand stays on the template with the people sitting around the table. "It requires imagination," she says, "and that is the stuff of stories."

In the hologram with the people around the table, a woman with twinkling brown eyes strums a harp. "Let the story begin."

Forest Guidance

Forest bathing is known to stimulate imagination and creativity. Beauty inspires us with impulses to create, to give back the note of our own song. Our brains thrive when we do art, which stimulates neural connections, so that we are influenced on a neuroaesthetic level.*

It's easy to be inspired to create art when we are inspired by the rich sensory surroundings of nature. All sorts of ideas for my writing effortlessly pop into my head when I'm out in the forest, including the story I tell in the next chapter. Perhaps it is the curvy, fractal shapes, the peace, or the way the countryside appeals to all of our senses. Go to a forest or your favorite spot outside and open up to any creative ideas that come to you. Ideas are not limited to writing, art, music, or dance. They can be mathematical, scientific, social, psychological, spiritual, or domestic, such as a new recipe, knitting pattern, or quilt design. Don't censor what comes, no matter how large or small. Sometimes it seems to me that ideas are circulating in the biosphere, seeking a receptive host. That might at least partially explain why many people so frequently come up with similar cutting-edge thoughts and inspirations. When we are in nature, we often experience an open and receptive state of consciousness that allows these flashes of humor, insight, intuition, and brilliance to land in us.

---

*See Yu and Hsieh, "Beyond Restorative Benefits"; and Magsamen and Ross, *Your Brain on Art.*

33
Sedna

We are in a time when the deep, dark, mysterious,
feminine life-giving powers are surfacing once again.

Sedna was betrayed. Her father cast her out of the boat into the stormy sea. She clung to the side until he chopped off her fingers. Then she sank to the bottom of the ocean.

At first, Sedna despaired. She thought she'd drown. Instead, she learned big magic from the depths of the sea, creating life from her severed fingers: dolphins, whales, fish, and turtles. Sedna became revered as a goddess of the sea. For millennia, she provided people with animals and fish.

But lately, Sedna found her powers diminished. Perhaps it was because of the changing climate, with oceans warming so that there were fewer fish. Or maybe it was because people didn't remember her anymore or feel grateful for the gifts she offered. Nowadays, all she did were simple tide pool tricks to help the seafolk, most of which Sedna figured the seafolk could do for themselves. She didn't mind helping, but lately Sedna had been longing for a vacation. Still, she hung her sign at the entrance to her sea garden: OPEN FOR BUSINESS.

After smoothing her seaweed hair, Sedna poured herself a cup of oyster juice. She peered out the window of her bone cottage, hoping that today wouldn't be too busy. Glancing at the long line outside, Sedna sighed.

She saw a shark with a sore tooth from too much chewing. She yanked the tooth out and the shark left it in payment. Next came a fish with loose scales, an octopus who'd gotten her tentacles stuck together, and a clam who was so clammed up he couldn't speak. The mask he'd been wearing ever since the pandemic was stuck to his face. Sedna shook her head. Silly creature didn't realize he was supposed to take off the mask at night. Most of her patients left whatever they had in payment, but she didn't charge the crab with the mood disorder. He was so depressed that he wasn't even enjoying pinching mermaids anymore! There was nothing in the rules about having to charge for tide pool tricks, although deep sea magic always required payment.

Last came a turtle who had lost her shell. Sedna held up a pink plastic bottle she'd found rolling on the sea floor and fashioned a new shell. As usual, the turtle, who liked to gossip, paid her with the news: the little mermaid was in love with a human prince!

"Oh dear!" Sedna said, watching the turtle swim off in a hot pink shell. A label stuck on the back had the word SEAFOOD written in glowing orange letters.

Closing up shop, Sedna headed to the surface to see what the mermaid princess was up to. The mermaid's mesmerizing voice swirled across the moonlit water. A young man leaned against a ship's rail and gazed at her. The mermaid begged him to join her in the sea, but the prince refused, saying that despite her beautiful singing, he would drown in the sea. "I'd marry you if you had legs and lived on land."

Sedna dove back down, satisfied that the prince could take care of himself. Even though it was late in the afternoon, there was still a line of customers in her garden. She treated a squid who couldn't quit squirting ink and a whale with a rather large bellyache. Probably another case of gut bacteria imbalance, Sedna thought, pouring probiotics into the whale's mouth. Sedna was tired and hungry when she called out, "Next?"

The little mermaid swam up. Sedna caressed her pet sea snail, wondering what she could do for the princess.

"Give me legs!" cried the mermaid.

Sedna shook her head. This was seal-pup love. And it would break the sea king's heart if his daughter left. Besides, Sedna wasn't even sure she could do it. Turning a tail into legs was deep sea magic, and that could be dangerous.

The mermaid princess didn't take no for an answer. She flapped her tail so hard that the bones on the cottage rattled.

Ignoring her tantrum, Sedna turned away. The mermaid shouted, "I'll tell my father you've hexed the kingdom. He'll throw you out of the sea!"

Sedna shuddered. If the sea king threw her out of the ocean, she'd have nowhere to go. "You'll have to part with your most precious possession."

"My pearls?"

"Your voice."

"Don't be greedy," she snapped.

Sedna tapped her long, gnarled fingers on the driftwood table, explaining that she wasn't being greedy, these were the rules; those requesting deep sea magic had to part with what they valued most or the magic could go hideously wrong. And, even if the mermaid did get legs instead of lobster claws or something worse, if the prince married another, the mermaid would be turned into sea-foam.

Nothing dissuaded the little mermaid.

It took all night for Sedna to make her brew. She sang over the boiling liquid, telling it of fields and flowers and walking on two legs. She was feeling faint by the time she took the mermaid's voice and added it to the thick burgundy potion.

As soon as she had the vial, the mermaid swam back to the surface. Sedna followed her and watched as she settled on the beach and gulped it down. Immediately, her beautiful tail transformed into two skinny legs.

The prince walked up and handed her a blue robe. Sedna watched him asking her questions, but of course the little mermaid could no longer speak. Sedna hoped he'd marry her anyway.

As soon as the sea king realized that his daughter had transformed into a human, he raged. The seas boiled and stormed. He was so angry that he even devalued the sand dollar.

Everything was so churned up that it was hard for Sedna to make it back up to the surface, and she couldn't concentrate. She gave the wrong slime-aide medicine to her sea snail and the poor snail broke out in purple spots. When the turtle returned—pointing to the hole in her pink shell and complaining that as soon as the sharks noticed the SEAFOOD *label, they bit her—Sedna felt worse. As she fitted the turtle with a new pop-bottle-green shell, she couldn't resist confiding about the potion she'd made. She knew it was a mistake, talking to a gossip, but the turtle was such a good listener.*

When the sea king dozed off and the ocean was finally calm enough, Sedna hurried to the surface. The first thing she saw was the prince on the beach. He was offering a wedding ring to a woman, and it was not the little mermaid. Sedna's heart sank. Even if the little mermaid was spoiled, she didn't deserve to be reduced to sea-foam. But there was nothing Sedna could do. It was against the rules to interfere with deep sea magic.

The shells on Sedna's bone door clattered as the mermaid's three sisters swam inside. That gossipy turtle had told them everything. They insisted Sedna save their sister. There was nothing Sedna wanted to do more. But for it to work, they'd have to pay with their gorgeous hair.

The sisters agreed. It was exhausting work for Sedna to forge the enchanted net. She added all sorts of rare materials, including the shark's tooth for strength and the mermaids' coppery-golden hair. When she finished, she gave the net to the bald sisters, instructing them to throw it over their sister before sunrise and she'd regain her tail instead of being turned into sea-foam.

Sedna was so exhausted that she could barely make it to the surface. When she did, she saw the mermaid's sisters toss the net. It floated high in the air before settling across the little mermaid. One corner caught on the prince and covered him.

Instantly, the little mermaid regained her tail—and her voice. "What have you done to him?" she cried.

Sedna winced. The prince had been transformed into a jellyfish.

The little mermaid followed Sedna back down into the depths, pointing at the jellyfish prince propelling himself along behind her. She pleaded with Sedna to change him back. But Sedna knew she couldn't. Deep sea magic was dangerous and unpredictable. Who knew what trouble she'd cause if she tried again?

The little mermaid threatened to tell her father and get Sedna kicked out of the sea, but this time Sedna didn't care. She should never have let herself be coerced into giving the mermaid legs. Feeling tired of using deep sea magic for trivialities—like helping women contort themselves out of their natural shapes to please and attract men—Sedna decided to go back down to the depths to find the real magic she once knew, the life-giving ability that created fish and whales. She put her pet snail into her pocket and swam down to the entrance of her sea garden. Then she hung up her new sign: GONE CAMPING.

Wriggling my toes in the sandy mud beside the little creek, I think about why that story landed in my head. Clearly, Sedna, known in mythology as the Inuit goddess of the sea, and my own sea witch version, represent the dark goddess: underwater, subconscious, submerged, and powerful. While at first, Sedna clings onto the boat, hoping her father will save her, he betrays her. It is when she plumbs the emotional, unconscious deep ocean depths of her psyche that she finds her own power.

Our tales often portray women with power as evil. Witches. But the time to reclaim our power is now. We do not have to give up our voices to be loved. Sedna has come back. A small reddish solar system body that takes eleven thousand years to orbit our sun was discovered in 2003 and named after Sedna.

It seems no accident that a solar system body named after a betrayed feminine goddess with life-giving powers is now coming to our conscious awareness. Sedna, my sea witch, and all the versions of the betrayed feminine represent parts of ourselves relegated to the unconscious but still life-giving depths. Men, women, children, all species, and Earth herself have been betrayed in this patriarchal system, which gives all the power to the rational, male aspects of ourselves.

Now we are in a time when the deep, dark, mysterious, feminine life-giving powers are surfacing once again. We are reclaiming all that was lost, co-opted, trivialized, and denied.

Still curious, I look around, trying to find the Blue Fairy Lady so I can ask her if I've understood the story, but she's no longer there. All I see is a shimmer in the air, the flutter of wings and swirling leaves twirling in a nonexistent breeze. "Are you still here?" I ask. "Is there more to the story?"

The answer floats softly into my mind. Maybe it is my own thought. Maybe it is the gentle whisper of the Blue Fairy Lady. "There's always more to the story." I catch a flash of blue in the branches before she adds, "Being in nature awakens your imagination."

Forest Guidance

What is it to embody your true nature rather than change it to get what you think you want, like the little mermaid does in my story? Without touching into our authentic natures, many of us are not even clear about what it is that we actually do want. I know that for a good part of my life, I was trying to read other people to find out who I should be, looking outside myself, interpreting cultural and social messages as best I could.

Learning to look within and come from our own truth brings us into the wellsprings of happiness and creativity. When we touch into these places, we may discover that our potential to co-create with Gaia may be bigger than we ever imagined. Since spending time in wilderness is so sensual, it is easier to "come to our senses" and be fully present. From this place of power we see what we see, smell what we smell, hear what we hear, and touch what we touch. We come to trust our own awareness and knowing, and this brings us home to our true natures.

Wherever you are in this moment, pay attention to your perceptions. What do you see, know, feel, taste, smell, hear, or think? How does it feel when you center your attention in your heart, gut, or feet? Take a moment to pause and feel into who you are in this moment. We are not fixed beings and constantly change as we grow through life. Knowing that gives me permission to be more honest with myself about how I truly experience each moment, rather than feeling like a failure if that truth turns out to be one of my less favorite states of being, like angry, anxious, upset, or sad. I've also noticed that when I allow and witness an uncomfortable emotion, it tends to alter and change.

34
Imagine

Sometimes trees speak in silence, in peace, in deep
relaxation that becomes communion.

What if we imagined the world we want?

How would we do this?

The universe responds to our frequency, the song in our hearts, and the truth of our beings. And there is nothing like being out in wild nature to uplift our frequencies.

So I'm off to camp in the redwoods, alone this time.

When I'm alone, I don't calibrate to another person's energy field. As I set up my tent, I tune into the big old trees. The clear clean energy sweeps through my aura, and I shake off any negativity, like a dog shaking off water.

It's a good thing too. I arrived not feeling very well. Not sure if it is a virus or exhaustion from a busy early summer season, visiting my granddaughter and going to my first big party in years. During COVID, I lost my social muscle and now find talking to lots of people fun but exhausting.

Anyway, I have a slight headache and swallow around a scratchy throat. It could be allergies. But I'm tired. As soon as the see-through mesh of my tent is up, I crawl inside to rest. Listening to the birds flitting about tweeting to each other relaxes me. The sound of the nearby river rushing down with so much snowmelt water soothes me. Dappled sunlight dances across my toes. Huge redwoods touch the sky above my little tent, and I feel sheltered beneath their boughs.

Lying on my thick pad, I wonder if what I'm feeling is the cosmic energy of the coming new moon and subsequent solstice. I've been clenching. Going over and over in my head things I've said or written, analyzing, judging, and seeing where I could have been more skillful. Some of the incidents are so petty. I'm sure no one else has given them a second thought. Why am I so overly analytical about myself? The answer floats in immediately. I'm still trying. Trying to be good enough, to be worthy of being here, and seeking validation from myself and others. I'm trying to be perfect in order to justify my existence. Am I living my life as a performance? This is such a waste of my time and precious life.

"Help me, nature devas," I whisper. "Wash my mind, body, emotions, spirit, and etheric being clean and clear."

Immediately, my whole body flushes with heat. Electrical currents flow up and down my spine. "Trust," whispers the breeze.

And I do. I let go so completely that I flop on my pad like a spineless jellyfish. I breathe like a baby, through my belly and down to the soles of my feet. I bathe in the deep felt sense of not being alone. All of nature is my ally. Nature wants our evolution as her own. She supports our natural growth. Past expressions do not need to be recalled. We can let go of imperfections, understanding they were the best we could manage in those moments. We can unfold organically, with absolute faith that our blooms are in the seeds.

"That's right," sighs a tree-scented gust. "Let life flow through you."

Drifting along with my waking dream, I see a black screw cap on the top of my head, where a baby's soft fontanelle is. When I mentally unscrew it, I watch a large white tapeworm crawl out of my head followed by some teeny white mealy worms. They feel like astral parasites inhabiting my brain. Maybe the image metaphorically represents tired old thoughts I no longer need, sucking down my vital life-force energy. Violet flaming the lot, I watch as they clear out along with a lot of hot air over things I've been all steamed up about. Feeling washed clean with the violet flame, I relax a little more deeply. In my mind's eye, a Gandalf-type wizard appears.

This is unusual for me. My interior mind-space is full of the Blue Fairy Lady, the Golden Lady with the Lion, elementals, and nature spirits. I don't remember seeing a wizard before. Why is Gandalf here?

"The sacred masculine needs to be owned and integrated. This is your ability to take action and have agency in the world." A loud confident voice speaks so clearly that I open my eyes and look around, trying to see who has spoken, but no one is around. It must have been part of the vision.

Stretching a bit, I yawn, thinking what a lovely daydream this is. It is so still here in the forest. An occasional little bird cheep-cheep-cheeps and that hum I sometimes hear in the trees, not quite with my physical ears, tunes up my cerebral hemispheres. It feels like the wise trees are expanding the neural capacity of my brain, increasing the connectivity between dendrites. I know we aren't supposed to be able to feel this, but there are little clicks in my head, and afterward I feel better. Marveling at how similar these neural connections feel to the networking threads of fungi, I think how often patterns repeat in nature. With the help of the trees, the hemispheres in my brain weave more closely together so that I can receive in a more holistic way. My headache fades. My stomach settles. Warm currents run through my body.

A golden beam of light flows from the crowns of the trees through my own crown chakra and down to my toes. I feel hooked up, like a battery being recharged. Letting my mind go into the music of the fluttering fronds, I gaze into the treetops and smell the sweet scent of mulchy soil.

Feeling more rooted, I can't help thinking about how uprooted modern people have become. Often, when we go down into our dark depths seeking the mysterious deep feminine wisdom, we run into our personal and collective pain. Here we find what has been shoved down, pushed out of sight, unseen—the nadir of our despair in the withered roots of the lost feminine.

Being with trees or any spot in nature can help us find the stillness at our roots. We come into resonance. We know ourselves as part of nature. We tap into our unquestionable worth. Viscerally connected, we have the wherewithal to allow what has been too painful to become conscious to surface. As these old, stuck energies move through us, we often discover sources of energy and vitality. Like Sedna, we find our power to co-create life and beauty with All-That-Is.

Allowing the trees to continue bathing me in their balm, I fall into a deep and restful sleep. The next day, I wake up and feel fine.

After a cup of tea and some oatmeal, I take off to hike up the Grove of Titans Trail, a newly renovated trail in Jedediah Smith Redwood State Park, admiring the almost translucent fiddlehead ferns, so fresh they glow with green halos. Climbing up past scarlet *Clintonia* blooms, white and buttery yellow iris, and occasional small pink primroses, I'm grateful for the good condition of the trail. Bridges are fixed and elevated boardwalks have been placed around the grove of gigantic trees. The boardwalks protect the forest floor, especially tree roots, from being trampled by too many feet. The renovation of the trail is a beautiful example of cooperation among California State Parks, Save the Redwoods League, Redwood Parks Conservancy, and the Tolowa Dee-ni' Nation. I love it that the Tolowa Dee-ni' Nation were consulted, as this area is part of their ancestral territory and they are the original stewards of the grove, which is a UNESCO World Heritage Site. For eight years I sat with these trees. They are powerful mentors and rain down starlight.

Lightly touching the bark of my beloved tree friend, I head back down the trail to find someplace quieter where I can sit for a while without being distracted by the conversations of tourists. Actually, I appreciate how quiet and reverent everyone is today. We pay homage with our silence to the sacredness of this grove. Passing a woman with a glowing, reverent face, I think to myself that she, too, is listening to the trees.

Sometimes trees speak in silence, in peace, in deep relaxation that becomes communion. Sometimes trees speak in soft whispers, in opening hearts, in waves of well-being and joy. Sometimes trees speak through rivers of wind caressing needles and leaves, sending messages through the atmosphere to the stars and cascading down to nourish mycelium-clad roots. Sometimes trees speak in sensations, knowing, even vision. And then we may wonder where the tree leaves off and we begin, where human and tree become one breath of life.

Forest Guidance

Do you remember a time when you felt so deeply at peace that you totally relaxed? Where were you? Was it somewhere outside, like a tropical beach or a garden? A friend who teaches meditation told me that when she takes people on guided meditations and suggests they find themselves in the most relaxing place they can imagine, most people visualize themselves somewhere in nature. Others see themselves in a library, concert hall, art museum, or in their home. It doesn't matter where the place is for you. To re-create the feeling of blissful repose, take a minute to remember that time of calm.

Do you recall any particular fragrances, like fresh bread, pine needles, or the scent of your favorite flower? For me it's the smell of the redwood forest, especially on a warm day when the air is redolent with earthy odors. What colors do you remember? The clear blue of a cloudless day or the deep green of an evergreen forest? Were there any sounds that were part of that moment? Waves crashing on the beach, wind soughing through the trees, or the laughter of friends? Was anyone else there with you? Loved friends, family, or pets? Recollect as many details as you can, and then create some of them in your daily life. Paint your room blue (or whatever color you remember feeling so great around), or buy a shirt of that color. If the smell of pine, cedar, or spruce is evocative for you, purchase one or more of these essential oils from a sustainable source and infuse your dwelling with the presence of the forest. If you envisioned an evergreen forest, perhaps plant a pine tree if you have a place to do so, or walk to a park that has pine trees. If a particular flower is part of your vision, put that flower in a vase. Sometimes a single flower is enough to bring back that sweet feeling. We can cultivate more moments of deep peace by noticing them and then re-creating similar sensory conditions in our environments. Sometimes our souls speak to us in silence, in peace, in deep relaxation that becomes communion. Sometimes our souls speak in soft whispers, in opening hearts, in waves of well-being and joy. And then we may know that we belong and that we are loved.

CONCLUSION

Dreaming the World

The time has come when whale songs
will sing through many of you.

The big old tree dreams through me. Words come.

Calling all whale singers, dolphin divers, turtle mamas, owl seers, lion lovers, and bear dreamers. Calling those of you who know you commune with mountains, rivers, forests, beavers, and birds. Calling those of you who do not yet know you commune with nature but will soon find out. Allow your open hearts to lead as you learn to listen to Earth. Earth can teach you. There is knowing in the rock and stone, the blood and bone, the bees and trees. The time has come when whale songs will sing through many of you, guiding humanity back to alignment. The time has come when the intelligence of Gaia will channel through you in art, visions, scientific inspiration, writing, speaking, gardening, singing, sacred activism, and presence.

The flow of words vibrating through my body, like the strum of a guitar string, pauses. Sitting, I gently touch the rough bark with the palms of my hands, stroke the solid trunk, and enjoy the coolness of shade and sunshine beneath the redwood's generous boughs. Breathing in and out, the hope that the tree's words gives me unlocks my grief and tears stream down my cheeks.

Slowly, the creaky words begin again in my head.

Follow along the wild path of nature. Dream the world you want into being, one small step at a time. Imagine crystal-clear waters bubbling merrily, refreshing you with every sip. Listen to the birds uplift you with their morning songs. Allow the flowers to warm you with beauty. See healthy happy children laughing and playing, safe, well fed, loved, cared for, and educated so each child's unique gifts can flower and blossom. Notice the animals, happy in restored habitats. Let your imaginations run wild. You can imagine the beautiful healed world because your souls remember. They remember that time that once was, when the world was a garden in balance. That time is past, and we won't return to it. Gaia is on her own evolutionary journey. All is a new arising. But we can include the elements that created beauty in that distant time to evolve new expressions.

Nature holds her breath, waiting for you to become conscious of your own divine nature. When enough of you humans do, and allow yourselves to be guided by Earth, miracles beyond your wildest dreams will happen.

Bibliography

Achenbach, Joel, and Victoria Jaggard. "In a Major Discovery, Scientists Say Space-Time Churns Like a Choppy Sea." *Washington Post*, June 23, 2023.

Aizenman, Nurith. "Fish Make Music! It Could Be the Key to Healing Degraded Coral Reefs." National Public Radio, June 15, 2023.

Andersen, Ryan. "The Eagle and the Condor Prophecy." Pachamama Alliance.

Aron, Elaine N. *The Highly Sensitive Person: How to Thrive When the World Overwhelms You.* New York: Carol Publishing, 1996.

Asgard, Scot. "The Tale of Thor's Wedding." *Asgard* (blog), May 31, 2022.

Baron, Nancy. "Salmon Trees." *Hakai Magazine*, April 22, 2015.

Behringer, Wolfgang. *A Cultural History of Climate.* Cambridge, UK: Polity Press, 2010.

Beresford-Kroeger, Diana. *To Speak for the Trees: My Life's Journey from Ancient Celtic Wisdom to a Healing Vision of the Forest.* Toronto, ON: Random House Canada, 2019.

Blackie, Sharon. *If Women Rose Rooted: A Life-Changing Journey to Authenticity and Belonging.* Gloucester, UK: September Publishing, 2019.

Caruso, Catherine. "Exploring the Science of Acupuncture." News & Research, Harvard Medical School, November 1, 2021.

Chowdhury, Madhuleena Roy. "The Neuroscience of Gratitude and Effects on the Brain." *Positive Psychology*, April 9, 2019.

Dacke, Marie, Emily Baird, Marcus Byrne, Clarke H. Scholtz, and Eric J. Warrant. "Dung Beetles Use the Milky Way for Orientation." *Current Biology* 23, no. 4 (February 2013): 298–300.

David, Gary. "Hopi Prophecy and the End of the Fourth World, Part 1." Ancient Origins, June 20, 2022.

Davidson, Ellen Dee. *The Miracle Forest / El Bosque Milagroso*. Illustrated by Carolan Raleigh-Halsing. Winterport, ME: 12 Willows Press, 2024.

Drouzas, Frank. "Segregated Sand, Florida's Beaches in the Civil Rights Movement." *Weekly Challenger* (St. Petersburg, Florida), November 12, 2021.

Eliot, Porter, and Henry David Thoreau. *In Wildness Is the Preservation of the World*. Los Angeles: Chronicle Chroma, 2020. First published 1962.

Emoto, Masura, and David A. Thayne. *The Hidden Messages in Water*. New York: Atria Books, 2011.

Evans, Zteve T. "British Legends: Elen of the Hosts—Saint, Warrior Queen, Goddess of Sovereignty." Folklore Thursday, June 21, 2018.

Furniss, Michael John. "Fundament Wonder." Soil Wonder, California Soils Council (website), no date.

Gagliano, Monica. *Thus Spoke the Plant, A Remarkable Journey of Groundbreaking Scientific Discoveries and Personal Encounters with Plants*. Berkeley, CA: North Atlantic Books, 2018.

Greenberg, Mike. "Dryads: The Nymphs of the Trees." Mythology Source, June 22, 2020.

Grossinger, Richard. *Homeopathy as Energy Medicine: Information in the Nanoscience*. Rochester, VT: Healing Arts Press, 2024.

Hicks, Maddie. "Treating the Blues: How Blue Spaces Have a Positive Impact on Mental Health." *Currents: A Student Blog*, School of Marine and Environmental Affairs, College of the Environment, University of Michigan, May 18, 2022.

Hunt, Elle. "Blue Spaces: Why Time Spent Near Water Is the Secret of Happiness." *Guardian* (Manchester, UK), November 3, 2019.

Jockers, David. "Improve Your Brain with Music." Natural News, March 22, 2013.

Jones, Adam. "Case Study: The European Witch-Hunts, c. 1450–1750, and Witch Hunts Today." *Gendercide Watch*, 1999–2002.

Kimmerer, Robin Wall. *Braiding Sweetgrass*. Minneapolis, MN: Mildweed Editions, 2013.

———. *Gathering Moss: A Natural and Cultural History of Mosses*. Corvallis: Oregon State University Press, 2003.

Leonard, Diana, and Dylan Moriarty. "The Science behind California's Extremely Wet Winter, in Maps." *Washington Post*, April 7, 2023.

Li, Qing. *Forest Bathing: How Trees Can Help You Find Health & Happiness*. New York: Viking, 2018.

Macy, Joanna. *World as Lover, World as Self.* Berkeley, CA: Parallax Press, 2007.

Magsamen, Susan, and Ivy Ross. *Your Brain on Art: How the Arts Transform Us.* New York: Random House, 2023.

Mandelbrot, Benoit B. *The Fractal Geometry of Nature.* Brattleboro, VT: Echo Point Books & Media, 2021.

Miyazaki, Yoshifumi. *Shinrin Yoku: The Japanese Art of Forest Bathing.* Portland, OR: Timber Press, 2018.

———. *Walking in the Woods: Go Back to Nature with the Japanese Way of Shinrin-Yoku.* Eugene, OR: Aster, 2021.

Morter, Sue. *The Energy Codes: The 7-Step System to Awaken Your Spirit, Heal Your Body, and Live Your Best Life.* New York: Atria, 2020.

Peltier, Drew M. P., Mariah S. Carbone, Melissa Enright, Margaret C. Marshall, May M. Trowbridge, Jim LeMoine, George Koch, and Andrew D. Richardson. "Old Reserves and Ancient Buds Fuel Regrowth of Coast Redwood after Catastrophic Fire." *Nature Plants* 9 (November 30, 2023): 1978–85.

Pennisi, Elizabeth. "Rare and Ancient Trees Are Key to a Healthy Forest." *Science,* January 31, 2022.

Pogacnik, Marko. *Nature Spirits & Elemental Beings: Working with the Intelligence of Nature.* Scotland: Findhorn Press, 1995.

Post, Anne. "Why Fish Need Trees and Trees Need Fish." Alaska Fish & Wildlife News, Alaska Department of Fish and Game, November 2008.

Preston, Richard. *The Wild Trees: A Story of Passion and Daring.* New York: Random House, 2008.

Ra, Kaia. *The Sophia Code: A Living Transmission from the Sophia Dragon Tribe.* Mount Shasta, CA: Kaia Ra & Ra-El Publishing, 2016.

Robbins, Jim. "The Genetic Power of Ancient Trees." Future Planet, BBC, June 28, 2022.

———. *The Man Who Planted Trees.* New York: Random House, 2015.

Shamas, Laura. "Aphrodite and Ecology: The Goddess of Love as Nature Archetype." *Ecopsychology* 1, no. 2 (August 1, 2009).

Shaw, Judith. "Elen of the Ways." Feminism and Religion, September 28, 2016.

Sima, Richard. "Why Birds and Their Songs Are Good for Our Mental Health." *Washington Post,* May 18, 2023.

Simard, Suzanne. *Finding the Mother Tree: Discovering the Wisdom of the Forest.* New York: Alfred A. Knopf, 2021.

Stokstad, Erik. "Ancient Redwoods Recover from Fire by Sprouting 1000-Year-Old-Buds." Science, News: Plants & Animals, Science, December 1, 2023.

Taylor, Jill Bolte. *My Stroke of Insight: A Brain Scientist's Personal Journey.* Hachette, UK: Hodder Paperbacks, 2009.

———. *Whole Brain Living: The Anatomy of Choice and the Four Characters That Drive Our Life.* Carlsbad, CA: Hay House, 2021.

Waters, Frank. *Book of the Hopi: The First Revelation of the Hopi's Historical and Religious World-View of Life.* New York: Penguin, 1963.

Weeden, Meaghan. "Orcas, Salmon, and Trees: A Film & Conservation Initiative." One Tree Planted, June 7, 2022.

Welch, Craig. "The Spotted Owl's New Nemesis." *Smithsonian Magazine*, January 2009.

Wetzel, Corryn. "Bizarre Fish Songs Raise Hope for Coral Reef Recovery." *Smithsonian Magazine*, December 10, 2021.

Wise, Caroline. *Finding Elen: The Quest for Elen of the Ways.* Scotts Valley, CA: CreateSpace, 2015.

Young, David E. *The Mouse Woman of Gabriola: Brain, Mind, and Icon Interactions in Spontaneous Healing.* Gabriola, BC: Coastal Tides Press, 2014.

Yu, Chia-Pin, and Hsuan Hsieh. "Beyond Restorative Benefits: Evaluating the Effects of Forest Therapy on Creativity." *Urban Forestry & Urban Greening* 51, no. 2 (April 2020): 126670.